The War Is Over
A rose without thorns

NATRAWN ROBERT WRIGHT

ISBN-10: 1492136107
ISBN-13: 978-1492136101

DEDICATION

This book is dedicated to the people of the world.

TABLE OF CONTENTS

NATRAWN ROBERT WRIGHT

ACKNOWLEDGMENTS

I would like to thank Mrs. Olive Rose-Steele for her guidance towards the completion of this book. She motivated me to never give up on my dreams. I would also like to thank my parents for believing in me throughout the years.

INTRODUCTION

People, you see the revelations of humanity in these days of tainted waters. These are the days which were written in the book of life, of harsh realities—history will never forget. People, I cry for peace among all nations upon the land of our forefathers. Across all the water of the earth the elements must unite the people of the world. Let all truths be told here and now about what's going on in this corrupted place, where human beings are supposed to call home in the universe.

  All wars end with this book. Life has already been destined for us even before we were born. I believe this and made it my duty to document world issues for you. The cycle of war continues and families have been fed for generations from it. The deadly process to peace allows many to live the American dream. Was it all in vain? Many lives are taken away in an instant blast and before your eyes the moment is gone. Must the cycle of humanity's failure of war continue? Ask yourself these questions because we should all feel sick to our stomach for allowing such great plague to infest our minds. Our innate understandings of the natural worldly laws should be upheld as our guide for peace and unity amongst the world population. We have failed humanity because we have failed ourselves and we are all to take the blame. This goes far beyond the races and nationalities that co-exist on the earth.

Think in terms of the entire world being controlled by a machine that we built. And the only reason why we are being controlled is because we are too scared of the machine that we forgot we built it and no longer believe that we can take it apart. These are world systems that I am talking about and it's closely related to voting in a democratic society. By no means am I saying that democracy is a bad thing so please read on.

In the democratic system, we vote our leaders into power to uphold their promises to the people to build better nations. What we see is that they turn around and change things drastically once in power. Think about it seriously, how I can say that for you, the masses, to know that we control the system and it is not the other way around.

What happens after we vote these leaders into office? They make laws to solidify their choices and form alliances that will guard their positions, but we find that these choices really separate them from us, and they brainwash us to think that we cannot change the policies that they create. Are these leaders' non-human or what? Come on now can't we see that this is what's going on all around the world, our world leaders separate themselves from us and so the masses think that they do not have a voice to change things that are not just?

Now, the international leaders do nothing about all the coups that are taking place in so many places in the world. The ironic thing is that most of these generals of orchestrating coups use democracy as the standpoint for their justification to overthrow their government. Can the international community do anything? Well, think harder because I am sure by now you know that the entity that was put into place after the League of Nations is now trying to do its job properly. Since the existence of the UN, history shows that this control factor exist even within greater established systems because we should know who really controls the UN. At times I have been disappointed with one or another Secretary General's for not trying to use their power to draw the international community closer to true commitments to make the world a better place for all people. Are those not true commitments?

In the past couple decades; I have only seen fear and sadness in their eyes. This is really how I view them and I have watched the UN do too little in many global issues. There is still great genocide happening as I write this and now it is 2013, a few years after arriving from

THE WAR IS OVER

Tokyo, Japan, after six plus years and living overseas. I have learned a lot about living with other cultures and had the great opportunity to compare the North American lifestyle and the Asian way of life. Now back in Toronto, I feel much energized so the reality of finishing this project is something that is currently in hands reach. I am also preparing to head to South East Asia to complete research studies on international living and education. Developing myself and my well-being is always at a constant for me so the idea of travel and working overseas is one of the biggest and most positive decisions I have made so far in my life.

     I am very happy that I was able to meet with a very special and inspirational Black woman. She was just like an angel sent you me from above with a message that was specifically for me. Finish it. This project deserves a grand audience on the global front. She is what her message to me was about and there is no better felling than to know that someone believes in you and what you have to say to the world. We met in a local Jamaican restaurant in downtown Toronto. If you love Jamaican cuisine, there are many local spots in Toronto to head to but on a Friday evening, but Diners after work is the perfect spot to relax, have some rum punch, and eat some of the best yard food courtesy of auntie and uncle. They supported me when I brought the actor Paul Campbell and artiste Everton Dennis, who were visiting from Miami and California, to eat at the famous Diners Corner. The Canadian premiere of the Jamaican film directed by Qmillion and Steve Johnson became a reality from this trip. I had seen the movie in New York and felt that the community in Toronto would love to see it as well. The movie is called Out the Gate, about a young man from Jamaica, played by Everton Dennis, who left Jamaica to head to America to make it big as a reggae artist and movie star. This resonated in my mind and I quickly familiarized myself with this young man as his story was a story that so many of us can relate to.

It is a lovely situation to be in the presence of like minded people who have great values and respect for each other, people who understand the cycle of life and respect the process. Musicians and other artists bring this energy to the table and like an interesting book; they are like magnet persuading others to believe in their cause. Surrounding oneself with these types of people was essential and it was then that I met her. Mrs. Olive Steele, an accomplished author and business woman. She later explained to me that whenever she visited that restaurant it was always a pleasant day because it was usually a planned event. She would enjoy a nice meal, introduce some folks to her books for sale, and then head off to get her manicure and pedicure. I felt that she was very deserving of being pampered and as I got to know her I realized that our encounter was perhaps the will of God. I needed a strong believer in the goodness of humanity to understand my mind. She is an artist who understood the powers of words and with some expertise advice and words of wisdom; she gave me a push to climb this great mountain. She wanted me to deliver my messages to the people of the world. She agreed with the ideas of sharing thoughts never to be forgotten.

First, I would like to say how wonderful it is to have great communication of a higher level with our elders. Many of my elders are still alive and they are so much in numbers that a thank you to all of them is essential. Names are not required because they all know each other. We start this process of thanking people in our immediate families. Everyone has a grand uncle who is always preaching something positive not only to you but to all members of the family. We can all relate and I consider myself very lucky to have some great elders in my family. When we meet people we feel their energy right away and for me, Mrs. Steele gave the energy as if she was one of the members in my family. Actually, the first person who came to my mind when I met Mrs. Steele was the famous Maya Angelou. She had the essence of a woman of great virtues, and the grey in her hair represented that of a wise woman with a world of experiences. It is with a warm feeling that I write this because I have been motivated by her to create a piece that the people can give great value to. As man she has guided me by helping me to balance my thoughts while giving her feminine touch, as someone who can also relate to a lot of the things I talk about.

All in all I guess there are always people in our lives who play the instrumental part and sometimes we do not realize this until it is too late. There are so many people of my past and present that I think about and being far away from home, helps me to realize that it is built in my DNA to always feel connected to these people. I think is has a lot to do with a people's bloodline. I have heard many stories of people walking pass or seeing someone that they had never met before but feel strongly connected to. It is like déjà vu, and I think it is safe to say that we have all experienced it at least once in our lives. The mere thought gives me courage to continue in my daily life. Why not do something that everyone who has ever been in contact with you can relate to? I made sure I took her advice and I started to write more and this time I wanted to be really loud.

THE WAR IS OVER

It is so easy to give up on something or put it off until another day. Then again there are times when there is a fire inside you and you know that the only way to out this fire is to do what your conscience is telling you to do. This is how I have been feeling lately. Then this lady reminded me that as new authors we must dig deep and put our hearts and souls into our work. We want the world of readers to speak to us just as much as we try to use our words to speak with them. She encouraged me to expand on my thoughts and say what is my true heart's desire and set myself free. This is what our lives should be about and I have learned that this is the power of writing. A level of documentation, great message, and the written or spoken realities should always be readily available for others to be reminded of who we were, our society at that time, and most importantly, our thought process and predictions of the time. This is a cycle that we must have respects for and it goes hand in hand with the fact that we need to end this insane cycle of war. I have been told that this is a perfect time for readers to read such a book. In reality, it has been the perfect time for the last ten years. It seems as if there has been continued bloodshed all around the world since the twin towers were bombed.

When I started to formulate my ideas to say something about war and peace, it was because there were wars going on around the world at that time. I felt that it became too entertaining and people were lost in the media stories not realizing the great atrocities happening in a world that is suppose to adhere to civil and democratic principles. I felt that I had to say something because I had friends who were fighting the wars and know of people suffering from wars in various parts of the world. We have seen Iraq, Afghanistan, Myanmar and other South East Asian countries, many West and East African countries, Israel, Palestine, Pakistan, India, Egypt, Libya, Iran, South American countries, the list goes on. Everywhere there is war and the world is infested by it. In 2008, I started saying to people that the world needs a revolution. I really believed it. But as in most major changes in life, there is a process and key events must happen for these processes to be enforced by us. All of a sudden I saw my words come to a reality and people were awoken to a new dawn of enlightenment. These were great changes that were needed and a great process that came with grand consequences.

We are destroying ourselves. At present we see one of the biggest conflicts currently unfolding, the Syrian conflict. The worst conflict that everyone dreaded has happened. It is a fact that Syria do possess biological warfare weapons and it is also fear to say that their leader at the helm, will use them as a last resort. It was even said most recently that evidence show that the Syrian army has indeed used chemical weapons on its people. Is this not the revelations of the critical times we are living in? If these rumors are true, then it is very safe to say that this is the beginning of another world war. We see North Korea threatening America and agitating war on a serious and large scale. Many say that it is just a strategy and propaganda spreading but the point of the matter is that at some point some general might not be getting what he wants on the home front and decide to hell with diplomatic strategies. Fingers are really twitching here and the world now looks like a time bomb about to explode and nobody really knows how to stop it.

What type of world are we living in? Aside from the physical war of manmade forces, there is no doubt that we are all fighting one of the greatest wars in all of humanity. This is the war of the forces of nature. Somehow, in the midst of all this fighting, we forget about countries who are trying to relocation their people because the land is sinking. Major flooding, thousands of people being washed away, homes, entire cities out to sea in a matter of minutes. Yet, as bad as that might sound, this type of war is not necessarily at the forefront as it should be. The leaders of the world really have their agendas messed up. I think this is why we are seeing uproar in the masses and images of revolution around the world in places we could not have imagined these things happening in our lifetime. Instead, we are still trying to hold on to things that is not ours, things that are material, and things that will not help our souls in the afterlife. As men we are still fighting for power, money, and for the stronghold of territorial grounds. We see business men in major multinational companies picking up and heading to the mother land.

They say that Africa is the new frontier for the world economy. Multinationals now have their eyes on Africa. They see resources before considering all the starving babies in many oil rich countries. Men will to leave their nice air-conditioned offices pack it all up and look towards Africa. Beneath all the smiles they are filled with greed and a capitalistic mindset. Drunken by these realities people taking this path easily forget that Africa has seen all types of vultures before yet they continued steadfast. Its young people are facing a new day of enlightenment and they will not accept colonialist business models any longer. But the problem is they have embraced the machine and danced with the wicked sisters.

There is still great hunger and starvation going on in Africa and many other parts of the world. Government

leaders continue to get richer and oil companies continue
to flourish. So it is easy to still see that most of the money
while came from the ground in African is still not getting
to the people who deserve it most. We still have major
problems as such and no longer can we blame outside
forces for these specifics. The leaders who allow this to
happen to their own people must be blamed. Any leader
in any country who will stand and watch as his people
suffers but goes home to a four car garage, a maid, and a
swimming pool, is robbing his or her people of their basic
human rights. It's sad to say that this is happening still
now and blacks are still dying while there leaders make
deals and fly in private jets with their white counter parts
who strike deals for more machines and more digging. So
come on, let's go and celebrate to the killing of your
people and eat their flesh as the same time. To me this is
what the grand steak represents, and I would rather die
than to accept these things. How could this be happening
still in these modern times of technology?

The world is sick. The media has a major disease
as well. Different agencies report only to satisfy the target
audiences and a lot of time forget the truth. Exaggeration
will always bring high ratings but what happens when
people find out about the truth. This is happening and we
lose ourselves in it all then go and watch a movie to forget

about it all. The system says its work tomorrow and it is all about entertainment in the first place. Do you not know many people have to die? Well as world sees it, there is no way that the world can sustain itself at the rate we are going so world populations must die. Governments cannot just point blank kill its people; they have to have a reason for it to seem justified. This is where we see sovereign states insisting they have the right to self determination so basically the ability to do whatever they want within their borders. The machine is out of control and you were told that it cannot be fixed so we are doomed.

This is why documentation is essential because it is the only way for future generations to know about the past. Never before in history have we seen so many people around the world rising up for what they believe to be their rights. They feel like their governments have been taken away daily from them and they do not know what to do. How can the masses of a country accept living in a situation when the people who they put into power do not want to hear their voices? When I speak about the machine that the people built, this is what I mean. Democracy is in a twisted stare and the global scene now looks like authoritative regimes flourish and finally the people have awaken and will not obey the rules. This is a very serious path we are taking so when we watch movies about the bad guy trying to gain access to weapons of mass destruction, we are trying to forget that this could be happening around the corner from you. Terrorism is around us and it's because of lies and secrecy why we are in this situation. This will continue and until world government start to develop democratic policies within their countries, there will more and more uprising around the world. This situation needs to be corrected at once. Developed countries need to tell the truth to the people that their privacy rights have been taken away. They must tell them that this is because of a bigger threat and the social contract is needs to be protected. What is happening is that governments take away our rights under our noses without telling us and this is wrong. Most people would not care if their privacy is taken because of terrorism, but when we are lied to about it, we can easily see that there is a serious problem and our democratic values are being lost.

We see that there is a big struggle happening within our society. If Edward Snowden felt that the masses must know that their lives are being secretly controlled by the government, living in a democratic country where civil liberties should have a voice? Then why should that same country prosecute him? Most people will look at the issue as clear cut as that. They will say within themselves that their rights are being taken away but at the same time if they are not doing anything wrong then they can live this knowledge. Is the government not supposed to give people the choice of knowing instead on keeping it a secret? This is where the point of me saying that they separate themselves from us comes into play. Once these secret laws are created behind closed doors, there is nothing we the masses can do about it. Or is there? This is the issue, we ought to know what the government is doing so there should never be closed doors when we vote our leaders into office.

It is also very essential for us to understand that the unwritten social contract between a government and its people goes both ways. In these critical times we must be able to look at both sides and make sense of it all. For example, America insists that these secret programs are needed for the protection of all citizens in the country, and in the bigger picture they are absolutely right. All governments have some levels of intelligence gathering and sometimes they need to do this against other countries, to be able to weed our organizations that are in search of blood without caring about hard working civilians who most certainly always get caught up in the fire. Intelligence gathering does help in the bigger picture because without it, all people in all countries will not be safe. We are all aware that there are groups that are dead set against government institutions and will brain wash and kill to get their point across. So, at times I know the tone of my writing sounds like I am against these institutions as well but this is not so. Trying to look at both sides of the border creates a balance and it is this grey area that we must all focus on. It is this grey area that governments must also protect by simply being transparent with their people.

There would not be so many great uprisings around the world if there was transparency in governments. Real democracy is as such where we are able to clearly see where our votes count. We should be able to gather information that is related to our livelihoods and make decisions in relation to policies that are there to protect these rights. At the same time this knowledge should also be present for us to make our decisions when it's time to vote. This is what we must fight for because we should not allow our rights to be taken away from us right in front of our eyes. Must we must also respect the system that helps to create a common ground for us to feel safe in our lives. With this in mind, my idea about whistle-blowers is that they their actions before and after they blow is critical to their justification for doing what they do.

This means that they have the duty of first getting all the support on the home front. They must build a case at home that will be so powerful that their government must approach the situation with caution, before directly labeling these people as traitors to their country.

Whistle-blowers who leave there own countries without getting the support from the people are less likely to be protected. For many people on the outside looking in, these whistle-blowers leaving their country because of fear for prosecution, shows some weakness and a lack of patriotism. People will not give them the full benefit and unconditional support because they are not standing up to their government like Mandela, or Martin Luther King did. These men did not fear prosecution and were willing to die for the rights of the people. Whistle-blowers such as Snowden have other motives that could be viewed as a stunt for personal fame. To outsider, they might agree with his position in terms of the sensitive information he release to the public, but his actions and movements does not support his claim for the love of his country. His actions instead made him look like a traitor who wants to give his country a bad name, while he himself claims international fame. In the end, his action might even divide his own country even more and worsen the countries relationship with other countries around the world.

      These are world issues that we are able to look at and see that a balance is needed for people to be able to have trust in their government while at the same time feeling safe that in their democracy, they can speak out against injustices without fear of prosecution. They are fundamental positions we must understand because it is directly related to war and peace. We see that the media can easily take issues and blow them out of proportion just for great ratings. This too can lead to war because one of the most powerful tools for regimes in these times is that of propaganda. The way information is viewed and shared should also have a balance. This balance relates to the common good for humanity not just for a people living in a country because ever country faces many of the same problems. Giving the greatest light to issues that can divide countries and create arms races is something the media must work on. The media has the responsibility of reporting without being biased in any way.

PART 1

WHERE DO WE BEGIN?

Oh mighty Father,

Let peace as the common good for humanity be upon all the
masses of the world

A light is needed to shine like the rays from the sun on the
living

A special force is needed like the one that helped build the
pyramids

To stop all the bloodshed from all corners of the earth

Let peace blast the world like the greatest rocket launcher.

A year ago, I read about a scandal. The scandal relates to
the issues of so many African nations. The money given
as aide to African countries to help the people never really
reach the real masses who really need it. Along the way,
someone with a certain level of power take control of the
money and this is where it stops. It is not necessary to
give specific names but it is said that the sons and
daughters of many political leaders in Africa, utilize their
powers the wrong way. If this is the case this must stop
because the outside world can clearly see that the millions
of dollars in aid send to Africa from nations from around
the world, never reach the real people in need. The

1

scandal was just one case out of the thousands of cover-ups and corruption happening each day. What we hear about similar cases through the media on these issues. Sometimes it is said that different rebel groups intercepted a shipment or stopped the aid from going to a particular destination. People are no longer buying it anymore. It is not right to live in a mansion and look outside and across the street you see poverty. This means you are an oppressor and your greed for material things outweigh the common good and virtuous laws relating to charity. This drastic contrast can be seen in many countries and we must look at this in a deeper sense. When we go deeper we realize that our minds have been plagued because we allow these things to happen right in front of our eyes. This scandal was not so surprising because we always hear about the children of world leaders and popular people getting into trouble. But when people's lives are destroyed or programs implemented to do good for people, we have serious issues.

When observing many world leaders I sometimes see fear in their eyes every time they give speeches. I always got the feeling that they take orders from someone with more power, as to what and how they must say things. I always felt that everyone took orders from the United States. The most recent war in Iraq at the time

when I wrote this was, for me, the perfect example where
we saw that America penetrated   immediately after the
inspectors were removed. At the time the UN should
have played a bigger role in terms of setting the stage for
the international community to be more involved. Yes, we
know that it was a touchy time for America. We should
also remember that the entire world was on their side
because the majority of the world still hates terrorism and
stand together against the people who orchestrate these
evil acts. If you agree with me so far or even if you do
not agree, the world now knows that there was no
weapons of mass destruction to be found. Most of us fell
into the trap because we were all so very shocked and what
happened. Nobody could imagine that America could be
attacked. So, nobody realized what happened after the
fact. For me it was not just a fight against terror, the east
against the west, Islam against Christianity; it was the
beginning of WWIII. Going back to the UN, it was clear
that the rest of the world did not have the power to even
give a world power alternative options of simple advice.
Advice to uphold the doctrines of peace and not an eye for
a eye. Would America have listened at the time? This
should be what true democracy is all about, the power of
reason. How can we say to others around the world who
consider themselves to be sovereign, to abide by the rules

of democracy when the biggest player brakes all the rules. Well most people would say that it was just bad timing and a very critical situation. If a sovereign state does not have to adhere to the principles of the UN under the treaties signed by the world powers, then our democracy is in fact anarchy. All I am saying is that everyone knows if the UN had been more diligent and determined to stop the war they would have flooded the places in question with more inspectors and foreign officials. That way it would have been harder for the Bush Administration to break the laws of the international system and of war, to attack Iraq. I wish the UN had more power but we will see later why they don't really have as much power as most people think.

On the whole, I do have a lot of respect for our political leaders and I hope they read this and perhaps now that time is at hand for our planet, being in office will be up soon and everyone will request to meet with me. This is what the Earthquake in Japan made me feel, like the world is coming to an end soon. When you think about it an earthquake of such a high magnitude that create cracks in the earth's core, I would most definitely have those among us who fight for knowledge to be documented, on my board of directors for the best initiative yet, The *War is over World Plan.*

THE WAR IS OVER

Hey please don't take this as a book written by a radical against political institutions and world systems, I am just merely exposing the dirty truth about what you and I watch and read in media every day. We as the masses must be able to speak loud and clear about certain injustices that affects our daily lives. Things that will affect our future generations because now is not different from the past and we continue to go around in circles. In the past, people stood and the only difference is that we are now fighting for different things. We are much smarter, and technology is at the highest point in history growing at rapid speeds beyond our imagination. Show we just allow corrupt politicians to lead us? Why should we be afraid to say what is right or express ourselves in a free world? I believe in democracy and some of the systematic realities show us what needs to happen in order to achieve true democracy and it never really ends up happening. We cannot think of the latter because that would be accepting modern day slavery on the grounds that we accept something other than freedom of speech, individual rights and free trade markets, for the world to come together and exchange goods and services, with the implementation of useful technology that we can access. Technology and democracy is just the perfect fit but the problem is that those in power use its fundamental ideologies of goodness and prosperity to grasp and hold on to the power, for that simple fact, power. That is all ok but when we forget the masses that are working every day in all the various corporations that make up the world, in the process, then we just fall into the uncontrollable machine that we can no longer change. I call this machine, THE MATRIX. Let's just say a movie; about 911 really motivated me a lot to say something to the world that I hope will never be forgotten. I am writing this as means of reaching as many people of the world as possible. This book is written from the core of which I am—the bottom of my heart.

The common good for the world is never out of my mind. Sometimes I sit and cry for the people of the world who are suffering, who do not have what we are so fortunate to have, a voice to speak freely, food, and a strong sense of self-worth. Regardless of what you believe or if you believe in nothing, please end this war with me the right way, right now in this moment of your time.

I use this term because in these times we all know so well about rockets and nuclear weapons. This is a great cry for humanity and I hope that you are not afraid to cry because your tears will not be in vain. I cannot compare my work to that of the leaders of our times, those from the past and those yet to come after my flesh has rotten and gone back to the earth, but I put the truth upon the highest heights and I know the world needs peace and not war in these trying times. This is the only way we as a people of the world can truly be free. I speak to all men and women from all walks of life, be not afraid to accept the truth into your hearts, as it will nourish your souls. Remember, none of the workers who worked inside the Twin Towers expected to meet their destiny on that day that history will never forget. So know now that peace is the only way like the reality we will never forget. We must find a way to break out of this insane cycle of life that we are all living. Listen, I don't care how conservative or conscious you think you are about the many problems facing the world, when I say we I mean we as a people. What the heck are we really doing to bring peace upon the earth? Can anyone say that we are trying hard enough? To some of the greats of our time such as, Grande, and Mr. King, trying to achieve great things on the grounds for humanity, includes great suffering. For us the suffering goes beyond tears to cry until you can no longer shed tears and think about what you can do to end this war. You are not alone because many people feel this way but now I want to make it clear that it is ok. Whatever level of resolve is needed, please believe that each drop from your eyes is the foundation that will stretch across all oceans. Are you scared? Are we naturally chaotic animals? These questions must be asked and you must try to find the answers first from within yourselves. This is the only way we will find ways to take control of THE MATRIX. If you don't know what the matrix is, it is the world in which we live. I use this term because we are so inclined to box office entertainment I figure this is the best way to get to you. I love action movies and I love the movie, the matrix, but for me it depicts such deep reality of the systematic slavery of our modern societies. These realities are what drive people insane and if you check the statistics you will realize that all across the world the rate of suicide is not declining.

It's difficult enough that the entities that are established to make good on these human problems, still allow international crimes to happen every day. Come on now think, we are rich in one sense, and we just love to buy diamonds and gold for our ladies and ourselves don't we? We will get into that a little bit more later but I hope you get the gist of where I will eventually go with this because it's not like you haven't discussed this with your family, friends, or in a history or politics class before. So let's start with Africa, being the cradle of civilization, as we know it. And while we are at it lets talk about black people and what their role must be in the entire process for peace and freedom for all nations. I am very disappointed with the entire black nation because I think we have forgotten how deep and strong our history really is, for the world and civilization on the whole. Black people are trapped in the matrix too, and we are so divided that we cannot use the same energies that got us out of slavery to influence the world to just face up to its self-destructive ways and actions. From there we can start to build a better way to the path of peace. We have forgotten the worship and respect of the sun, the energy of life for the earth. We have forgotten the deep significance of our history relating to kings and queens and slavery and the unending stories of faith and power and determination that has saved us to prevail over all evils since the beginning of any documented history as we know it. We have forgotten that we were the ones who built the pyramids with the might of divinity rights. We have forgotten that our ancestors communicated with the sun the moon and the stars. We have forgotten the great inventors and the fact that even today the greatest mathematicians cannot figure out how it was possible to build the pyramids. Black people need to play a bigger role to unite the world. We must bring back our souls, the light that protects all men. We are too lost with our modern day riches that we forgot that there is still slavery in Africa and systematically in all parts of the world. I say this because there is no doubt in my mind that the black-race is greatly influential to the world and can change it. We are all Africans according to modern day findings. All nations are one, like the great philosopher, Sun Ra, who wrote about the elements all being the same; I believe this is so for people no matter color or nationality. Like water, air, and fire, we are the same upon different degrees. My standpoint is that black people as a nation, should take part in these major international issues. This means playing the role of the peacemaker. We must all look at these major issues, such as war, modern day slavery, genocide, and play the great mediator for the world, for our brothers in the east and in the west. I stand strong with my belief that black people can change the world for the better. Remember, the black race has never fought against any other race, only amongst each other. Can the black race play a bigger role? This is not an easy task, but who is willing to try? I feel that this is going to take a long time to happen considering the fact that we can't find a way to unite ourselves, as black people. Statistics in America shows that one of the main causes of death for black men in America is black on black crimes. Now, let's not look at Africa because the guns that the blacks there are using to kill each other are from America, and some European country, how ironic. The divide and conquer method of control established by the Romans and later by imperialistic doctrines of Great Britain and Spain, really raped black people of their identity and souls. I still feel that until the black race unites as one people there will always be war upon the earth. This idea must be seriously embedded into your thoughts because history will show that the blood of the black race has stretched upon all nations, so unity is our only option. Take it as you wish but you should search deep so you might know and understand. What's happening in the world today can be looked at using the stereotypical black family structure as the prime model. What do you know of the black family structure? What you think you know is just the reality you see in most the inter-cities of America, and other parts of the world. What you see is that there is a high crime rate and you see a lot of single mothers, and people on welfare. Do you think these situations were derived from rational choices? With these issues, choice is just minor politics. By no means do the media make anything better because their shows, magazines, and TV programs would not have high ratings. So what we see are people just judging and limiting their understanding of the black race from stereotypical propagandas and thought. We must search deeper if we want to get to the roots of it all. Also, please trust that it is all relative to the world condition where all nations are involved. The black race was not destroyed by a mythological system; it was infiltrated with divide and rule method of control. We see this happening in front of our eyes today as well. If America were able to successfully bring democracy to Iraq, we would see this formula in motion again. The problem is when trying to create the divisions, we must be prepared for a civil war, and this is what has happened. These formulas were developed to be implemented rewritten and reviewed for generations. In the end the same systematic formula used against blacks, manifested into a self-reliance world machine and is now biting chunks out of the world. On the surface level, just look at our lives, we work all year just to get that two week vacation so we can find ourselves in Jamaica, listening to reggae music, and contemplating if we should get some weed from the herbs man to cool our CNN migraine. The only thing that holds most of us back is fear, the fear that when we get back to work there might be mandatory drug testing. Regardless, it is the best two weeks of our year yeah, our vacation. Now say thank you to our wonderful systems that we built that has now enslaved us systematically, welcome to THE MATRIX.

The motivation to share my thoughts about the realities of

war is what makes me write although I still question myself as to what held me back in the first place. I now realize that it's not about what was holding me back, it was the fact that the process is continuum and everything in between is the life we live to survive and all the trials and tribulations that we go through. So writing for me is a most powerful tool along with music, the players of instruments and, without contradicting myself, when I wrote that these political leaders want to hold on to power once they get into office, this is like the power of word of mouth as stories of the lost tribes continue and DNA findings are proving some truths many were scared to believe. Now I see more on television the young generation preaching the things I have been writing about for years now. I listen to music and I hear some of the best artists such as Nas and Junior Gong bringing some of these realities to light. I felt the feeling deep inside of me but now the situation has gone too far. Now even within myself I wonder how many times this feeling has gone through the minds of so many young intelligent leaders of the world trapped in the urban metropolis, seeing the home front and the world front being torn apart by our so called "leaders of the world". Where are the real leaders? Are you not a leader? Just the other day ten young souls lost their lives due to the likes of intercity violence as families come home to watch glorified world affairs of young boys and girls with guns. You all know what I mean when I say this because you see it in the news all day. It is not difficult for the world to see the truth and know what is going on in our society today. It is just that we run away from acceptance of what is happening so it's impossible to make a change. I want to make it clear that the analogy of our world systems being looked at as a machine that of which I called the matrix started when I started writing this book. I realized that it was an ongoing project and I decided to revise it because the first version seemed to be too radical in terms of direct name calling and so on. Name calling is minor as we all share one planet and must take responsibility for its demise. But even in this reading I still want you to think and drawn your own conclusions for ideas looked at. What is the outlet for us? So we instead go to the movies, fishing, or hiking up north every chance we get to forget about everyday life. Seeing pictures of small children with M16 guns in their hands, chaotic visuals used as product of propaganda. What is the meaning of this all? Why are many leaders of the world glorifying war today? Have we not learned from our mistakes of the past to realize that war is never the answer and it should never be a last resort? I know that many people will disagree but its ok, we should all know more about the ethics of war and peace. For me, it's all like the thin line between love and hate that we walk every day in the system. Just walk the path and keep your balance as a way to say we naturally must have a clear knowledge of who we are as a human beings living within a system. The role of race and the different outlooks associated with these topics, have such great value because thanks to technology we can no longer pretend about some astonishing findings. The only two things we know for sure are that we are born and we all must die. But do we really die? Our ancestor left many traces for us to understand what is happening—the world needs to be replenished. That doesn't mean we should kill each other, does it? At the end of the day the system is designed that only the strong will survive so it is essential to form cells and alliances within the matrix the same way in which politicians use their influences to safeguard their positions. I try very hard to make it all sensible but also for people to think and gain knowledge of understanding of self as a source of energy for life.

We now know that the world population is high and our consumption is too outrageous to sustain the earth so I believe the core of the earth is cracked far worse than any scientists can even proof. My feelings cannot be overlooked because on a personal experience note, I felt the large earthquake was coming in Japan far before it physically happened. Many people can attest to the fact that I spoke about my feelings that something very terrible was going to happen and in fact I had dreams. Dreams I spoke about to close family and friends. The questions may go on about the end of the world as we know it and I believe that there are many answers that lies within Africa, America, Europe, and Asia, let us cry for peace for humanity because only a handful of people in terms of the masses of the world, control the system. All nations must work together with Olympic standard synchronism, but are we all doomed anyways? Ask and you will know the answers from within and with this book. This is the only reality I know and it is our own history that has taught me this.

Think in terms of the "double victory" ideology that plagued every black man even before times of the Tuskegee airmen. These were some courageous pilots who lead the way for the final thrust into Berlin, Germany, during the Second World War. It was not only the Tuskegee airmen who experienced such conflicts within, but this mindset has plagued the nation since blacks arrived off boats from the mother land and even after some of his truths are being revealed. It is the mind from within that speaks the truth, the one that shows us who we really are. Now with the aid of continuous modern day findings, eastern history, and the understanding of African history, we should all know that black people play an important role for the entire world build up. It is quite sad because we ourselves have not yet grasp such great understanding deeply as we should, for us to know that until we unite as a people, there will never be peace on the earth. The sources are so vast and the truth will always be told about a stolen history that will forever be the secret story that ought to be told. Still, now the war must stop and we need to know that the answer is simpler than we are programmed to think or believe otherwise.

Thinking about the stories of king and queens and their divine riches are merely the surface of these truths. Many historians would bluntly say that the western civilized world as we know it used the divide and conquer method of control to destroy a people's history, only to reap what they sow, and now we see that war has plagued us all. Like the forbidden entry into the grave of king Tut, only to steal his gold and riches and not thinking about his afterlife. Well at that point they found a statue of the boy king who was black and perhaps it fits with the biblical stories of a time in Egypt which is linked to Joseph and his brothers who were Hebrew Israelites. Even in these times of great technological advancements, we have again found ways to give grounds to one school of thought that human beings are naturally chaotic. I tend to look at the other school in that, it is simple to see how humble babies really are and we cannot forget we were once babies, as humble as can be. Are we civilized? What human practices determine how civilized we are? While not trying to prove a point to you I am speaking from self. We must always have questions about the world around us. So over the years I have learned that we need to know history to understand what is going on in the world today because we are only creating great genocide amongst ourselves being in the matrix together.

Have we embellished so much into evil doings that we glorify and romanticize war? Just look at your television set and it is there for you like a war game video game or a movie special reflecting on the making of the civilized world as we bring order with the creation of chaos. If we are really so
civilized then what is all this fighting for? Are the security dilemmas and the various arms races weighed greater than human rights and freedom across the world? These are the things I want to touch on these days from the smallest issues that you might think to the biggest. For example, you know it really bothers me when we throw so much

food away, because we should always be thinking about all the children and people around the world that need what we throw away. I guess the fact that we throw so much away shows our values in these chaotic days where materialism means everything so we rap our souls and throw it away without even thinking. Yeah I think about these issues that are considered low politics. If you are asking yourself why I am writing these words for you, well, let's just say we are all living in the city and the concrete jungle is as real as the Bob Marley song.

I will be happy when I know that people all around the world carry my book in their gym bags, to work, to read on their thirty minute break, wherever and whenever you have guts to be brave and free your mind just a little. My words are not stolen and I want you to take it as a gift from me to the world, prophecies that are so simple for you to grasp and start to make changes for the world to be a better place. This is a new testament on the realities of the world, as we know it. You have all heard babies cry; well this is a cry for peace moving like the wind with the might of great prophets. The story of a world that is lost with hatred and war over and over again. I see visions from a far and sometimes I feel like my ancestors are talking through me touching your souls and mine at the same time. This is why I write for you, words that people may read and find the truth or even themselves in the process.

Am I afraid you might ask? Well as much as I might say I only fear God and no other, I know that the world will hear this cry as it comes with the might of humbleness, like a child who cries for hunger. This is more like a great starvation to see peace on earth before I die. The truth I have seen every day thus far. Do not get me wrong I love my life but I hate going off track and the point of it all is learning from our mistakes that we have made over and over. It's just that being young and so caught up in wanting to find answers for our human condition and well-being, I see society on the whole as being a big rat race. Concrete jungle or not, this fighting has got to stop. We cannot blame everything on the corrupt leaders of the world because we have ourselves to blame for putting them in such a position in the first place. There is corruption all around us like a plague. Can't we all see that it is time to make major world changes before it's too late? This is where I am showing you that my writing is a process and in my editing I had to interrupt because as I write now back in Toronto, I feel more that the third world war is at hand. I did a mini music project called

world war three theory years ago and now looking back I
have realized that I have been feeling the earth for a very
long time at a very young age. We know that historically
there has been corruption in the world even before Christ
and Judah, the eras through the beginning of modern
times as we know it. The blame must be shared equally
by all for allowing such hatred to penetrate and infest our
minds, especially people of power who are responsible for
the lives of the world's citizens. We must start to make the
appropriate stance from within our homes. We all just
seem to be out of control these days. Look at our society
and aspects of our well-being, chaos is present at all levels
and it affects the masses that do not have a voice. I want
to be that voice for those who are scared to say what is
right for the common good of humanity. We need to find
a way to end all wars in the world. Why can't the powers
who sit on the general assembly do anything about the
great genocide that is happening in Africa now as I
continue to write and develop this revised version, THE
WAR IS OVER in 2011? Or, has a third world war already
started? It is almost 2012 and there are many predictions
that the world will end soon. Would it be ok for us to say
that soon could also mean another 200 years or more? I
am still trying to put it all together right now. A black man
is at the helm of America while we still talk about the fact

that we did not think it would happen in our lifetime. Meaning we really do not understand the cycle and the time at hand. The reality is it was time for the man to take power and the world welcomed it. They are looking towards the man for hope to free them from their sins against his forefathers.

This goes back to the issue of the Black man. His role in the entire equation is that his decision is essential to the outcome of war and peace on the earth. The black nation must unite if there will ever be peace on the earth and this is such a big issue because the black nation is so divided. It almost seems impossible for our unity on the whole to be realized and so is the case for peace in the world. Both issues go hand in hand because black people are such an influential nation on earth. Check your history and you will know these facts. It is our responsibility to unite as one race and work towards uniting the rest of the world. It is our divine duty to do so but we are too lost and scared to grasp such great understanding of who we really are as a people, and our calling on earth. They have been used to build America and the rest of the world, plagued by the divide and conquer rule, caught in a trap and we have drunk the wine of the wicked. Many black leaders around should be ashamed of themselves because on a day-to-day basis they let their people down and the rest of the world. They have accepted the position of being used as puppets to fulfill the evil works for the same nation who raped their mothers, hung their fathers' fathers, before they were even conceived. I am not against America people; I am just saying the truth. America is still the best country for the American dream but, is this the dream of our human consciousness? Black people you are still here, now what will you do for the world? We were supposed to be extinct like so many species that we are now finding are so closely linked to the cycle of life and the earth on the whole. First you must understand that I am only entertaining your eager to search for more to nourish what you already know. Now I feel like we are getting somewhere. Sharing ideas and philosophical views with the world is the greatest of all freedom. That I am very proud of doing with you now and it has been a long time coming. How can we separate our personal lives from our inner self? What I am trying to tell you is that I have done this because my inner self speaks with unlimited life and such energy I feel is aided by the invisible angels flowing around the living. I have not forgotten about the souls of the past and I have channeled what I feel is real for people to think about. I had to let go of the fact that my life is not perfect and I have made many mistakes but I have learned a great deal in the process.

As I write with spirits of the most high, I steer out my window, I look to the sky and I wonder. I wonder about all the souls out there in the east fighting for something they don't even understand, it is now nightfall in the east and a war is going on. I wonder about soldiers on both sides of the fences and I think to myself that there are only a few real generals left. These are the leaders who will go on the front lines to protect what I am saying and tell the young boys to step back and die so that they can develop strength. Strength not to fight but to realize that the fighting must end. I once asked my father how we could stop all the wars and corruption in the world. I never knew my father to be a religious man, but he replied by saying, the only thing that can stop all these happenings in the world is called "divinity intervention". I looked at him and I smiled because I did not expect him to go so deep with the truth, the depth that we are so scared of. The generals are all caught up in trying to gain stripes on their shirts while forgetting about the realities of peace and happiness. Instead, they chose to dwell in the art of war. But who are the true generals? Is it the man sitting in his office reading Sun Szu or ON War? For me, it's quite fascinating to know that I sat in class with some of the people who were waging war for Bush and continue to fight for our freedom to exist. Yes it is that bad, and its way beyond religion and the races. At this moment as I write we are currently seeing Obama as president of America and in two weeks I will drive to Vermont for my 10th year's college reunion. Looking at the past when I was a young university student, the mood at that time was quite fun and I remember, professor Andrews, telling them that they will be the ones to fight the wars ahead of us. Now they are actually doing it and I am happy with my position of being able to document a part of history that must be written for the consciousness to continue to live within our minds. I am sure many of my ex classmates didn't quite know what they were getting themselves into until they actually got there in the arena. They do all this training for war so I am sure at times fingers might twitch because hands want to feel the real thing but is it the right thing to do? I have since learned that war is a business with rules like any large corporation. All I know is that bombs don't know how to say sorry. This is what many sign up for and they are brave and fearless in action and every sovereign state needs such mind to compete in the world.

To know your future you must look at the past. Soldiers,

like Black men, are put into positions to be used as puppets for the political world. Just look at the political world and the leaders that are in some of the major roles. You might realize that some of these leaders use blacks for positions such as advisors and their minds are brain washed from that point on. Others who should hold an international stance are left by the way side when their decisions are not for the common good of the world but rather that of a scared boy in the playground whose only way of survival is to become friends with the bully in the school. This is what we see happening in our society today. Black men are continually being used as the token souls who are still lost from their truths. Their own teachings are being used against them and they fail to see because we are blinded by diamonds that original Hebrew people buy from the Jewish man in America.

If you look in various parts of Africa today you will see that black people are still killing each other to provide riches for the rest of the world to lavish. Is this not the greatest of all crimes? Is there not an international body for these crimes that are being committed? The truth is that there is such an entity but the body has fallen into the belly of the beast. That is the plight black men must face today. Historically, he has been so divided that he is blinded from the truth and does not know how to find it.

Those of us who try to be above the surface can only blaze fire upon Babylon with the words and the thoughts that are here to set you free.

Take these words now and let them be the light of your salvation, the words that only you can understand in your own way so you can find truth from it. I speak to you with the angels from a far singing in my ears that I must write for my youths to know the truth. This is not just for the understanding of ourselves or the demons that have captured us; it's a reality we cannot forget. It is a representation of what is deep inside that is driving me to write. This book is written for you to free yourself with just one thought so please don't take this as a black panthers diary, the ideas and principles that are upheld herein was intended for all nations to be fed with the bread of the earth. College kids throughout the world should discuss these issues in their social, history, and politics classes.

I want to present to you my essays. They include issues of the Second World War, peace, race conflict issues, social order, America in Post-World War Two, and events discussions as a chronology of World War Two. The central theme to this book flows around the idea that the

black nation can bring peace upon the earth but it is so
hard to be realized because of systematic divisions that has
turned into a self-reliance machine I call the Matrix. This
machine now has systematically enslaved humanity and
now the people want an revolution. What I can say is that
I hope there is not a World War Three even though I have
already stated that I feel it is happening now. But the way
things are going anything is possible.

I want you to know who I am and what I stand for.
We must not always look at the picture just for its physical
representation but what its mere existence means to
everyone who views it. I love the world so I write this
book for every seed upon the earth. Sharing my mind
body and soul with you means the world and everything in
it, deeper than the Scarface movie. Come into my world
and I will share my thoughts with you but do not be so
judgmental. Don't be afraid of what you already know
from within, the things about yourself that you could
never explain or put into words. Are we really such
mysterious beings? Or are we just too scared to face up to
what we know about ourselves? Let us set ourselves free
from the usual nine to five mind set, without forgetting
that it was all a part of the plan in the first place. As a
black man I have seen the rise and fall of every great
power of the world since the beginning of existence. We

always played a role and now it is time for us to play a bigger role to unite for the world to be free. That is the only way, or our seeds will continue to war against each other. I look at our brothers in the east and I know that we are still in bondage but now the plague has infested minds and once again we failed to understand what Richard Wright and W.E.B Du Bois wrote about and felt in their times of enlightenment. We don't even get the essence of what they saw and the issues they predicted for the times.

I consider this my gift of enlightenment for the world. We have allowed ourselves to become biased to only look at one side of the spreading propaganda. Forgetting what history has taught us about ourselves. We have committed crimes against ourselves. So, I guess you could say that I write about much of the things that are plaguing us as a people in this civilized world. I also like to swim back to the surface from time to time so I don't want to contradict myself. This book will involve papers that I have written over the years on various political, social, historical and modern issues. I hope somehow I can put it all together so that you can make sense of it and learn something that you did not know before. The first story is an introduction to the international system and the rest are a

reflection of my documented research within the
international studies core curriculum. They uphold
historical facts of different social issues such as, major
world events, war issues from the past to the now present.
My thoughts and ideas should help you to look at the
world for what it really is, a place where its people are lost.
I started writing this book in Toronto Canada before I
decided to move to the other side of the world. Now I
live in Tokyo, Japan and I must say I like it. Coming here
has changed my life forever. I have realized that it has also
helped me to get a good look at the North American
society from the outside. I think this has helped me to be
more balance with my thinking. Please enjoy this book
and try to get as much information you can to help in the
fight against all wars on the earth. We need to protect the
earth for our children. It seems to me that all generations
do things out of impulse, without thinking about the
future when we are all gone. We must not forget that when
we die we would have passed on everything to our
children so why not make it good and positive. Break this
insane cycle, now the war is over.

PART 2

UNDERSTANDING EVENTS THROUGH
HISTORY AND SYSTEMS

It is essential to get some groundwork understanding about world political systems and how they work. I believe my essays, exams, and historical chronologies will help the reader get a better outlook at how the political systems of the world control the masses directly and indirectly. How can we the people of the world gain our strength back to unite the world and stop all wars? The answers are within us and we need to constantly be aware of our surroundings and understand the major issue that's happening in our world today. Once we are inclined to the causes of wars and conflicts around the world then we are able to look at ways to prevent them. I think the only way this is possible is for the masses of the world to join together and stop being followers of a system that controls the masses. It starts within your household and at your work place. From within self we must try to figure out what we can do as individuals to unite ourselves. It is sad that we are so scared and we as a people of the world no longer believe in ourselves, this is why we venture off into watching movies like the matrix knowing that we are essentially living our lives in the matrix. How can we find our way out? It is not as difficult as we think sometimes so we must stop thinking one dimensional and understand that one person can bring forth many changes if such individual believes what is right and is willing to die for such standpoint. This is why we run away from such reality and we say to ourselves that we are only one so we cannot bring by changes. Ask yourselves, who puts our world political leaders into office? When you realize the answer then you realize that the masses are the ones with the real power to stop all wars and bring peace. The problem is that we are too divided through nationalities; religion, worldly positioning, and lack knowledge and understanding on an international level. This is why education is so important in these times because one without such worldly understanding is not able to bring by changes because there must be a starting point. Here the starting point takes a brief look at International Law. We will be able to get a better understanding as to why the UN may seem powerless, when it comes to solving certain international issues. People will say bad things about such establishments that are put into place to deal with major international issues however, when we understand better how the law works then one can realize that sometimes the UN cannot interfere so easily into the business of a state that considers itself a sovereign state. Other issues must now be looked at relating to NATO and their positioning in the many different areas around the world. These deployed groups need to fully understand their influence and objectives wherever they are placed. We are able to see that at times there has been many problems with the NATO troops and once they are not trusted by the people, and feared, then the problems then become worst. When looking at systems we must relate them to technology in that they must always be updated and renewed. I think this is what must happen with the UN. Their objectives need to be reestablished and cater to the world for the benefit of people who need help and genuinely trust the establishment. We will briefly look at the way that the UN works. We can see and it's quite disappointing that the power of such an establishment does not have enough to fully satisfy the objectives of the peace process. This is why the importance of policies needs to be upgraded and reconstructed for the best possible formula that works. If and when these changes are made, the world will see and know the results. This is what must happen because whenever the masses of the world are not happy then things should change. Is this not what politics should uphold for the people of the world? My essays will touch on some of these issues in a more in-depth manner. This is for a better outlook and understanding, as my thoughts are sometimes biased. A balance is provided through facts about these issues, documented for the benefit for higher inclination.

Let's Look at International Laws

When looking at war we see that states have considered it in their sovereign right to wage war against anyone who was considered a threat. As war was thought to be a characteristic of the international system, it was looked at as being natural because all states within the system felt that they were entitled to engage in war as a right through the principles of sovereignty.

This is why states believe they are entitled to use force against other states. It was a way for them to protect their sovereignty, in the sense that they are protecting their territorial grounds, their independence, while defending the state and its people. War would be an inherent part of the international system because states make up the system and states needed to enforce the law themselves. A role of war is the fact that it is also used to make laws as a way of establishing new systems. Powerful states do not want to recognize any authority above them, and so the nature of the international system is characterized by anarchy where

35

there is no central authority or international policing to enforce the laws. This is where we are able to say that sovereignty is a basis for anarchy because in anarchy, states are responsible for themselves.

The ideas of self-help short of war come into play because states should be able to use self-help techniques to get other states to do what they want them to. This is where we see powerful states using their power of self-help in order for other states to comply with them. In such situations, states may face problems as a result of using their self-help techniques. These problems involve the ideas of perception and interpretations. The fact that states make their own laws and enforce them, leads to the fact that they also perceive and interpret their laws the way they see them fit.

This may cause conflicts with other states because states perceive and interpret laws differently. This is why we are able to relate power with the law in the sense that the more powerful states are able to make the laws and enforce them even to the extent that weaker states must comply with these powerful states. If weaker states do not comply with the powerful states, arms races may occur when states feel insecure when other states arm themselves. This causes the security dilemma and in an international system that is characterized by anarchy, no one is left secure.

Theoretically, in such a situation, a balance of power may be the result that in essence may prevent wars and conflicts from occurring.

The differences between legal and political disputes is that, legal disputes are justifiable meaning that there is a question of law and such law is relevant to the dispute and can be utilized to settle it. Political disputes are non-justifiable in which non-legal considerations (such as "vital national interest"), plays such an important role that the application of legal rules would not settle the dispute. We may also realize that these differences of disputes also depend on the attitudes of the parties involved. If any of the parties seek only their legal rights, we see that the dispute is classified as justifiable, as being a "legal" dispute. The opposite would be the situation where one or both of the parties demand legal rights and also the satisfaction of some special interest that would require changes in the legal situation, then the dispute is non-justifiable, being a "political dispute".

These ideas show that the international system may have its weaknesses with regards to the legal system. This is because in the international system there is no central authority to enforce the laws and so legal disputes may be over looked. This is because states are not bound by the international system but instead they are bound to themselves. In trying to settle a legal dispute through the international system, this may even cause more conflict because states may not agree with laws of such a system and so it would not be enforced because states are only bound to themselves.

These problems relate to the very nature and characteristics of the states, which comprise the system because states make their own laws and enforce them. They do not have to comply to any other authority but themselves being that all states consider themselves to be sovereign with a right of self-determination. This is how we are able to relate these legal dispute problems in the international system to nature and characteristics of states because states make up the international system and they are also the enforcers of the laws within the system. Even though states sometimes view a decision based on law as a good way of settling disputes in the international system, they do not always choose to adapt such views because they comprise the system and are only obligated to themselves as sovereign entities.

The fact that a large number of modern armed conflicts have taken place without an official declaration of a state of war, armed conflict has been used as the term of such conflicts. The idea of "international armed conflict" includes conflicts between states and any international legal person. The Security Council that is comprised by states decides if the UN should engage in international armed conflict.

They must all agree that the UN should use force to accomplish a common goal, end a conflict, or create stability. The logic of this system is that states that are members of the UN get the opportunity to be heard before the Security Council deploys UN troops. Each state feel that their opinion on the specific situation is a valid opinion with considerations that they have these rights, they are rational, and are acting under the principles of sovereignty. This may cause many problems however, and it goes back to the idea of perception and interpretations that states do not always agree. The fact that they are all members of the UN does not mean that they will agree with the Security Council or the other factions of the UN. This may cause the international issue to become more serious with regards to non-interventions, interventions or simple neutrality by the UN. This is where we are able to see the inherent problems in the system because even as members of an organization that encourages peace, we see that these states still disagree with each other. Major decision making such this international armed conflict poses many conflicts within the organization. This may lead to other conflicts or even another world war.

We cannot forget that the world is governed by systems. They are systems that we have created and they give guidelines to all the world powers to suggest and make laws within their territory or sovereign state. The issues have always been the idea of enforcing a law after it has been through all the processes and is enacted. There are so many particulars that stems from the bodies and establishment surrounding these laws. The main idea however is to know what the percentage or possibilities are for a just and right law to pass all the stages and manifest into reality. Usually it is easy to know what Laws should or should not be pass, just look at the consensus of the people of the world and you will find your answer. This is why clearly we can see that America is losing the war against terrorism. We can easily see the consensus of the world and the reality is that the issues are no longer weather Iraq had weapons of mass destruction. The results of this recent war which in fact, is still happening as I write this, is that the consequences are far worse than perhaps what America had expected. There is a huge undertone that puts great pressure on race relations and the ideas of religion, specifically, Islam and Christianity. The war brought out many issues that are so far away from fighting terrorists and finding weapons of mass destruction. We must not forget now that war is so influenced by politics in these times. Such standpoint is quite important because there is no longer the ideal war that is waged as in past centuries. Politics brings rules and regulations to war which means that weather we believe it or not the heads of these sovereign states waging war against each other must communicate on issues or fighting against each other.

PART 3
ESSAYS ON POLITICS

Preamble

There is no particular structure to these essays and as
much as I tried to put them in order I found myself
thinking that it is not quite necessary. The idea here is not
to really prove one essential point to my readers but
instead to give factual information on highly philosophical
issue studies, world events, for a better understanding as to
how we operate as human beings. The essays do have
some sort of order but it is not really as important as the
issues I am trying to cover and if it gets too confusing at
time please try to understand as best as you can relating to
the things you already know as facts or relative to the
various issues in this book. As you read on you will realize
that I have tried my best to link the essays for it to make
sense to the readers while my objective from an
educational standpoint is for the reader to gain better
understanding of systems, politics, major world issues,
black people and the roles they play for the entire world. I
am doing this without trying to be biased because I am
black. Clearly I have pointed that my people still have
major issues that needs to be addressed in order for us to
help the world unite for peace. There is also not one
particular country that must make things happen. The

world problems deserve and need the collective unity of all countries. There are many issues that will be looked at but one must not forget that the main issue is the cry for peace. College students must learn and discuss the many ideas of this book and that is why my essays play such an important part. My ideas are separated from the included historical facts and this should allow the reader to enjoy my writing as simple and straightforward as it is, while looking at the educational points as well. Next we will look at why war is limited by politics.

War and Peace

War is a choice made by political leaders. They make these choices to benefit their states and protect their sovereignty. We are able to see that the objectives of war relate to those of political leaders who make these choices. The choices they make may depend on many different factors however, we see that their choices usually deal with their sovereignty, where by states try to preserve themselves in times of war and peace. This shows that politics and war are both concerned with interests and both are concerned with the power struggle, rules, regulations, norms and values as a way to feel secure and maintain order. As war is about creating order, politics makes sense of war by establishing these objectives. When objectives are

43

established, the perception of the opponent should be considered because it should be important to try and know what the enemy is thinking in order to fully understand the situation at hand and satisfy these objectives.

Decisions to accept terms are political and should be seen as states always wanting to achieve their objectives in war and peace and using politics as a way to do so. This is where the saying that war is the continuation of politics by other means, a statement made by the great soldier and philosopher, Carl Von Clausewitz, comes into play. This is the understanding that politics is a way for states to conduct wars with different types of forces. These forces involve the entire social structure that is influenced by politics as a way of waging war against other states. These ideas manifest themselves through treaty laws, economic sanctions, trade relations, and other political forces. While relating these ideas of politics, war, and peace, and why the decisions of political leaders influence the outcomes, some thoughts must be considered. It is the idea of how people think and perceive things. The first approach is based on the assumption that humans are inherently violent creatures and that the civilizing veneer of society is all that saves us from chaos and self-destruction. By contrast, the second approach rests on the assumption that humans are inherently peaceful beings, endowed by nature or God with an innate desire to cooperate and nurture. These thoughts, right or wrong, may cause many problems when trying to understand war and peace, and why people make these choices. They limit political leaders into thinking a certain way that might influence their political decision-making pertaining to whether war or peace will be an outcome for the state.

It is difficult to define war and peace and the factors associated because everyone does not have the same thoughts about these subjects and they perceive them in different ways. The factors are endless however; we are able to limit these thoughts while looking at specific definitions, and understanding of war and peace. First we could look at the idea of the ideal war. Historically, war has been around since the beginning of civilization. For Clausewitz, the ideal war is absolute unlimited violence and bloodshed. This is the only real rational war. This is the situation where by political rules and regulations do not apply. There are no considerations that would limit bloodshed in the ideal type of war. In contrast and as ironic however, this idea could also be a way to limit war and attain peace.

This fact that war becomes so violent in its true nature, leads to the idea that people would be unwilling to fight wars. If this is so, then we are able to see that political leaders and states limit the ideal war through politics.

Politics comes into play because it is the component that is used to limit such wars through means of rules and regulation of war. This is considered to be the modern system because the conduct of war is still prevalent however; politics considers and inflict war upon other states in different ways from the absolute violence and bloodshed. There arose, therefore, an endeavor to establish principles, rules and even systems for the conduct of war. Thus a positive end was set up, without keeping properly in view the innumerable difficulties, which the conduct of war presents in this connection. The conduct of war has, as we have shown, no fixed limits in any direction. Every system, every theoretical construction, however, possesses the limiting nature of a synthesis, and the result is an irreconcilable opposition between such a theory and practice.2

This was the endeavor to establish a positive theory of war as a way to better understand it, in trying to prevent it. States would still conduct war but it was a lesser violent type of war where we saw laws pertaining to war being applied.

As a way to promote peace and better understand how to achieve it, we could relate the positive theory to that of the social structure of peace, which indicates that peace, must be "social" because it involves cooperation and understanding. Fogarty explains that we think of war and peace differently because of the two schools of thought stated above. He explains that peace can be achieved in a number of ways depending on one's point of view however; many states maintain peace through the "balance of power" between them. This is the best that states could hope for because decisions of war and peace involve states and the security dilemma.

Once there is a balance of power, states feel safer and the result is peace until a state feels threatened by the other and then the process must start over again. This is the event that ensures that no one power in a region has so much power to be tempted to inflict war on other states. With a balance of power, states realize that the neighboring states have also maintained their power up to par thus; the unwillingness to fight becomes more prevalent. This is where we may see peace as an outcome of the balance of power with relationships between states. The absence of war happened through the political processes where political leaders decided to have relationships with other states knowing that there is still a security dilemma.

We must look at politics as a way of limiting war and as an obstacle to peace. The processes of the balance of power is a way for us to see that states do not want to fight wars, instead they would much rather limit it by using politics to do so. As a way of limiting war, we must realize that politics causes a source of friction in the sense that it distinguishes real war from war on paper. This is the idea of friction, which shows the involvement of politics in war. Politics limited the idea of the ideal war and this is how it is seen as an obstacle of peace. This is also where we see it as a source of friction because war on paper is very different from reality. Theoretically it sounds very well: the commander of a battalion is responsible for the execution of the order given; and as the battalion by its discipline is cemented together into one piece, and the chief must be a man of recognized zeal, the beam turns on an iron pin with little friction.3 These events are looked at as processes of how the conduct of war ought to be from the political standpoint.

In reality however, these processes do not always work because once in war, the danger that it brings intensify the evil so greatly that they must be regarded as its most considerable causes. We can relate outcomes of war and peace to the choices made by political leaders because outcomes good or bad have always been a consequence of the political process. From this we may realize that even though politics may limit war and can be look at as an obstacle to peace; the understanding of the concept of peace must be involved if these political leaders want to use politics as a weapon. If we look at the ideas of "positive peace", we must also look at that of "negative peace". Only by looking at the two sides may we better understand these two phenomenon. Starting with the negative thoughts of peace we see that a positive outcome shows the irony in it. "Negative" conceptions of peace can be troubling, because using them to understand the human condition seems to lead to a paradox: that peace can be achieved through war.4 These ideas also show that politics may be used to cause wars just as much as it is used to prevent it. When politics is used to achieve peace, the political leaders consider the ideal type of war which in its true nature, lead people unwilling to fight. This is a way to achieve peace because everyone would realize the level of destruction caused by the ideal type of war. "Positive" definitions of peace seek to be more comprehensive. The mere prevention of war, or negative peace, is viewed as a limited goal at best, because it does not address many of the other forms of structured violence that are so prevalent in the world.5 In looking at this we may say that that peace, may be achieved through war or simple the processes of trying to achieve it.

The obstacle of positive peace is that it is social because

it involves cooperation. It incorporates the processes of politics that utilize its power. By doing so we see that there are states must be willing to cooperate in order for the peace process to be effective.

We must understand that many states and political leaders may choose to disagree about what peace really is and because of this, it then becomes difficult to decide whether or how it can be achieved. It goes back to the ideas of how people perceive and interpret things. If it was simple to say that peace can be achieved through simple agreements among people and states, then ideas of values and norms may be seen. Three categories for peace could be looked at, they are: Agreement, awareness, and understanding. These concepts deals with ideas associated with social theories that try to create peace through cooperation. Cooperation that starts in every community within states and leads to international recognition, while keeping values of natural laws, a norm that sets precedence among all nations.

These are some of the ideas of the social structure of war and peace, where theories of how to understand this phenomenon and achieve peace are looked at. Fogarty explains these theories and tries to make better understanding of them. Like Clausewitz with the ideal type of war, Fogarty also presents an ideal that deals with the thought that we may never be able to fully realize positive peace. This is because we see that politics limits the ideal war but it does not result in positive peace where wars no longer exist. The situation where we see states living in harmony, where the struggle for power no longer exists. The ideas presented relates to the fact that the best we can hope for is a balance of power where states feel secure. This ideal represents the idea that human beings are interested in peace.

This is why we see that the ideal war would not happen in today's society. The political systems have changed from times where we see waging war of the ideal type.

The idea the human beings naturally want peace and use politics as a way to get it by limiting the ideal war, leads us to look at some methods for promoting peace. These methods are social in the sense that they involve communication and cooperation. One general direction these efforts have taken is the application of deterrent force; military might sufficient to discourage the military adventures. This is an approach fraught with risks, especially as weapons have become increasingly dangerous and increasingly available to small nations. This basically shows that the efforts that are been made to promote peace, still involves many risks that may still cause conflicts leading to war.

A second form of this effort has been to expand the "peace group" that is, to form larger states, coalitions and empires that include larger populations within them. The collective security afforded by this approach both increases the strength of the group in question and reduces the potential number of adversaries. The third approach is to bypass the state as the sole actor in the conduct of war and peace. Citizen diplomacy and civilian national defense are ways in which the inherent barriers to peace posed by nationalism and statehood can be diminished.8

These are methods for achieving peace and we may find that problems may occur from these decisions because even though they may have some effectiveness, they are not way of achieving "positive Peace". This sort of peace is a matter of predictability where we see the trust in one's fellow citizens and in the future. These ideas relate to that of the second school of thought that explains that human beings are naturally peaceful.

The idea of positive peace gives the notion that it will naturally be attained. Where it has been tried, it has almost failed, as can readily be seen in much of Africa today, for example. Instead, the peace of predictability is best achieved by creation and maintenance of justice, and this is only achievable nonviolently.9

The creation of justice is also a way for creating peace.

This is because justice is the mutual reinforcement of cultural ideas and social structures that are able to set examples and lay foundations for peace. These considerations could also be related to politics because it is this system that decides the laws and regulates them. This is an obstacle to positive peace because justice is considered a universal idea that involves politics in its processes. We must understand that regardless of the many methods used to try to achieve peace, positive peace will never occur. Factors that limit this is also the fact that war are limited through politics meaning that there are in fact many different types of war, which differs for the ideal type of war for Carl Von Clausewitz.

Ironically, one of the obstacle to positive peace is politics even though it may also be an obstacle to war. This is where we see that Fogarty's ideal that we may never be able to fully realize positive peace should be considered. All the above factors shows that war can only are limited by means of politics and the choices made by political leaders. The best we can hope for are limited wars as an outcome of politics. We know that the ideas type war will not occur because of its violent nature, and that positive peace may not be attained. States then are left to make their own choices that will influence their relationship between other states.

This is where we see that the balance of power could be the best possible outcomes because it involves states that want to feel secure. If every state tries to balance their power, then we see that peace is the result. The topic of war and peace brings many considerations because it is so broad. In trying to get a better understanding of why the two concepts are so highly discussed, we had to define war. The idea of the ideal type war is used because it is considered the only real war. We saw that this type of war may not be achieved in today's society because politics limits it from happening. This brought the idea that people would be unwilling to fight these wars because they were too violent. Even if such limitations make war more palatable, the mere fact that the ideal type cannot be achieved shows that politics limits the "progress" towards ideal war and is considered an obstacle to peace. We saw that the obstacles to positive peace while still promoting peace may not always work. An example could be seen through justice that is an obstacle to positive peace. It is absolute because different states perceive and interpret justice to fit their traditional values and norms of the society.

Even though we may never be able to fully realize positive peace, peace in general is still important. We could also look at it as the absence of war in a state as a way of showing that human beings are really interested in peace. This is the idea of the United Nations that represents the world on a whole through its members. The United Nations was formed at the end of the Second World War as a way Unite the world by promoting peace internationally. If human beings were not interested in peace then such an organization would not have been formed in the first place.

In knowing that human beings are interested in peace, we know that they would find ways to limit war or stop it. We cannot however, stop war for good because positive peace could never be achieved. This is why states who political leaders to make political decisions that will limit the ideal war.

Once the ideal war is limited; politics has played its part as being an obstacle to peace. These are the ideas that were looked at and show that war and peace go hand in hand. We must not forget that they have been around since the beginning of civilization. Many have tried to better understand these two phenomenon's through the studies of many different theories on war and peace. It is very difficult to fully understand the ideas of war and peace and why these choices are made. We do know that political leaders make choices that cause war. Simply it is to understand that states do not always agree and this could lead to war. In today's society however, wars are limited from absolute bloodshed and violence, which was seen in wars of the past such as the Napoleonic wars when the political system was much different from today's system. All these factors come into play and this is why the subject is so difficult to understand. We can conclude that from the many historical changes in warfare, that human beings are interested in peace. They are not willing to fight the ideal war because it creates such vivid thoughts of chaos that people naturally will not accept. The most important thing is that states feel secure through the balance of power. This is the best case we could hope for. Once everyone is secure then they feel secure and there would be no reason to go to war thus; peace is the result.

The Washington Arms Treaty

Photo courtesy of: *GlobalOpsAnalysisCenter*. N.p., n.d. Web. 23 July 2013.

At the end of world war one, Japan and the United States got into arms races. Great Britain was also torn between both countries because of their involvements in the Pacific. The United States government were embarrassed that the world knew about their conflicts, and the apparent fact that the citizens were unhappy did not help at all. Great Britain influenced the United States to call a disarmament conference. Washington sent invitations to the specified countries. These countries were: Great Britain, France, Japan, Italy, and lesser power as well.

This was the Washington arms treaty of 1921. America made a plan for disarmament with regulations of ships in the Pacific. They wanted to find a way to stop arms races so that both parties are satisfied. Everyone did not agree with the plan made by the United States. This created the four-power pact. They were: The United States, Britain, France, and Japan. They all embodied certain principles, which they all agreed upon. They wanted to respect each other's rights in the region of the Pacific. They also agreed upon a joint conference to make whatever adjustments needed. A level of communication with one another was also established. They had to inform each other of other countries that might pose a threat to any of them.

At first the different countries seemed satisfied about

their agreements but there were also disagreements as well. The nine-power treaty relates in that it was a culmination of years of American policy in the East. It was also set by certain fundamental principles that became international law, binding upon each signatory. These nine countries were The United States, Great Britain, France, Japan, Italy, Belgium, Netherlands, Portugal, and China. The agreement was on behalf of China who had been violated by these countries after world war one, with regards to commercial open door policies. They violated China's territory so the contracting parties agreed to respect and support the sovereignty, independence, territorial, and administrative integrity of China. No other treaty or agreements should infringe upon these principles and they also agreed to respect china' s neutrality and consult fully in circumstances requiring the application of the treaty.

Japan's three main objectives at Versailles

At Versailles, Japan three main objectives were to see that their demands to the former German islands were met without any interference from British dominions. The first of the three demands were: asking for cessions of the islands in the north Pacific. These were the Marianas, the Carolinas, and the Marshalls. The second demand was for a confirmation of their claims to the former German rights in the Shantung province. Thirdly, Japan asked for a declaration of racial equality among states. This was in fact in relation to one of the basic principles of the League of Nations.

These claims, especially the demand of racial equality by Japan, raised a huge protest from Australia who was of the British Dominion. Japan's claims to the islands violated the principle of annexations because these claims were somewhat going against the new ideas associated with Chinese Nationalism. The officials who represented Japan on these issues were confident about their demands, mainly because they knew it was their legal rights to make these claims. After all, the island was captured by them and was in their possession. The fact that Japan also demanded for racial equality was in turn held by high moral principles. Japan's claims were met by European allies and by the treaties and notes signed by China.

The way in which the claims were sustained was by secret concessions by these allies. Even though China did not want to sign the treaties, three years later they gave consent to the transfer of Kiaochou to Japan. They in turn wanted Japan to restore leasehold to them, even though they would maintain Germany's economic rights in the province. Countries such as the United States did not want to see Japan expand but they knew that Japan had legal basis for their claims. Eventually, none of these allies who wanted to block Japan's expansion were prepared to challenge them.

The Marco Polo Bridge Incident

Japanese troops occupy the Lugou Bridge.
Photo courtesy of: People's Daily Online, all rights reserved.

The Marco Polo bridge incident was one of the major hostilities between China and Japan. Fighting broke out between the two countries and their forces. The area was important because of the Peiping- Hankou railway, which was very important in relations to advances and machinery and transportation of goods. The Chinese government authorized foreign commanders to drill troops in the region. In turn of this, it was like an invitation for big trouble.

THE WAR IS OVER

Japanese troops went to the Peiping area and demand that Chinese troops withdraw South of the Peiping area and Tientsin. This demand was refused and led to Japan taking over with their troop. The Japanese emperor wanted to start negotiations but China decided they could not tolerate further interference of their sovereignty in the region. They were prepared to bear arms and in response, Japan too resorted to arms. Japan stopped any efforts to control the area through economic and political pressures. Japan eventually took over the region of Peiping and Tientsin. They destroyed China's main Line of overland communication with Russia. We saw that Japan invaded China on major fronts. Both parties did not want to lose their integrity. The Japanese navy was so strong that they had an advantage over China, one that they used to the fullest. They seized islands from China, blocked their shipping ports and limited their territory. Japan also forwarded a series of peace proposals involving Japanese control of Chinese areas, recognition of Manchukuo, and the formation of an economic bloc of China, Japan, and Manchukuo. Japan eventually failed to conquer China as well as bringing its government to acceptance of peace.

Japanese troops during the initial fighting after the Marco Polo Bridge Incident
Photo courtesy of: Paradox Interactive, all rights reserved.

An Analytical Essay--China and Japan (1916-1937)

1937 Japanese marines invaded Shanghai.
Photo courtesy of: Torikai Lab Network, all rights reserved.

The developments with China and Japan between 1916 and 1937 went through many different changes. Both countries faced changes in the social, economic, and political situations of their countries. We saw that Japan, like China, was always in transition of new governments and governmental policies, social transformation territorial capitalization. China went through social transformations especially through reducing the commercial and industrial role of the great western powers. We also saw that Japan took more to the western world and their new ideas in development and innovations, while China tried to stay as neutral as possible. They knew that if they try to compete with the new ideas of the west, they might pose a threat from Japan as well as the west themselves.

With regards to military power, we saw that Japan became far more powerful than China. They had the third most powerful navy in the world. While Japan strives to maintain and gain military power, China on the other hand faced many problems within their government. China was torn in trying to function between ideas associated with the past, particularly Confucianism and nationalist government. They had a bad socio-economic situation causing the migration of sons and daughters to the cities to earn money for the family to survive. They had cheap labor, long hours, and extreme exploitation of female and child labor. This is when China's started its first labor organizations. Japan in contrast saw the future of their commercial and industrial expansion in the membership in the League of Nations. They wanted to develop a policy of conciliation and adjustment to China's new nationalism. Japan was also more active than China in the field of arbitration and adjudication of international disputes.

Japan and China went through many other changes in their development especially in the areas of territorial regimes. We saw that Japan and china were always in conflict over different treaties and policies regarding territorial boundaries. Japan went through a period of government responsibilities in the world while China tried to develop with the new world and these new ideas of capitalization, liberation. While Japan was going through a continued expansion of their political and territorial standpoints, China went through major social transformations, and an internal revolution regarding Soviet communist policies and the ideas of the new world of capitalization and liberation. These were some of the development between the two countries, China and Japan between 1916 and 1937.

PART 4

BLACK FIGHTER-PILOTS IN WWII

I would like all to know that war and peace is about humanity and the common good for society. It's about black people who should play a larger role in the entire equation. I am a black man and I am really trying to play a big part. I have expressed so many different ideas and I have realized that my emotions and personal life has been affected because never before have I expressed such deep feelings to anyone even within my family. I just can't sit back and watch what's going on around me and feeling powerless. I want to change the world through my writing and I hope that this is possible every time I start to write. In relation to war, my next essay talks about a group of black pilots who lead the final thrust into Berlin, to end the Second World War. There was in fact a movie made about these men however, to the extent of their great contributions, more should have been said. These are the types of men we need to bring forth peace on the earth. They are the type of men who can sit at the bargaining table with terrorists and come up with suitable and effective solutions. We need people who are not biased looking for the best for their race or country, but instead see the world and its entire people as one with world unity at the forefront. These are the brave men needed to fight and win the war to be won. "It is quite ironic that our brothers in the east are looked at as, sand niggers". I wonder who came up with that idea.

The Tuskegee Airmen in World War II

During World War II there were many men who were forgotten. Some of these men were known as the Tuskegee Airmen who made contributions to the war and the victory of the Allied forces against Germany. The issues faced by the Tuskegee Airmen during World War II brought questions of how were they able to overcome racial problems and successfully complete bombing missions over strategic targets in Europe. The Tuskegee Airmen were African-American pilots who went through many obstacles to achieve success as fighter pilots in the war. By getting the chance to exercise their skills, their superb flight training, determination, and willpower, enabled them to complete their bombing missions in Europe, while making history as the only squadron who never lost a   bomber to the enemy.

During World War II, the United States faced rigid patterns of racial segregation that was not only seen by the civilians but in the military as well. Black military aviators were trained at an isolated training complex away from the white military aviators, near the town of Tuskegee, Alabama. This was at a time when African-Americans did not have the same rights and privileges of whites and the rest of America. Many questions can be asked about such facts in American history especially that of these black pilots who wanted to fight for their country even thought they were not accepted by the same country they were fighting for. A lot of their determination and willpower came from the fact that they had to prove to themselves and the United States that they were great pilots, some of whom already had their civilian pilot license, who deserved the opportunity like any other American, to fight for what they believed in.

This research will analyze and interpret these issues faced by the Tuskegee Airmen, starting with the issue of the experiment known as "Smoke Screen". This evaluation will also include issues such as their racial problems on the home front, their situation on the battlefront, and their victories during World War II. These issues showed the many different situations they faced, during their training and even in Europe. The ventures of these Airmen started when the War Department, after being criticized by the NAACP and various newspapers, decided to conduct an experiment called "Smoke Screen", at the Tuskegee Airfield.

In looking at the details of the experiment known as "Smoke Screen", it was obvious that this was one of the many obstacles that the Tuskegee Airmen had to overcome. There were however some high officials such as Judge Hastie, a member of the Supreme Court and a civil rights activist, who wanted to see these black pilots integrated into the Air Corps training centers with the whites, but because of the policies at that time, this was not possible. The thought was that higher morale could be established if blacks and whites that were going to fight together could also live together. There were no doubts however that desegregation was not going to happen and thus, other means had to be taken. Basically, the officials in the War department expected the experiment would prove racial deficiencies in intelligence and concentration. Officials such as Judge Hastie, who opposed the experiment at first, reevaluated his decision because the experiment was the only way the War Department would allow these black pilots into the Air Corps.

In early January 1941, Judge Hastie withdrew his opposition of the Air Corps plans. He felt that the inclusion of African Americans in military aviation, even as separated squadron, was a positive action, and a situation that could be manipulated, over time.

This showed an effort by a white official to influence the War Department into continuing the experiment hoping for success and perhaps even desegregation in the Air Corps and the rest of America. The War department would tolerate no mistakes because it would result in the dismissal of a pilot or perhaps even the experiment on the whole. Even though the War Department was continuously being criticized by factions such as the NAACP and various Negro newspapers, their policies on segregation and discrimination in the Air Corps and the Army Corps was still in effect.

The criticism from the press and the public towards Washington were considered justifiable because this went on during such a critical time where we saw black pilots, the Tuskegee Airmen, struggle to be recognized as effective pilots able for combat and fight for the same country that treated them as second class citizens. Washington and the War Department showed their hypocrisy in advocating unified national defense against the fascism and racism practiced by the Axis members, while ignoring America's own racism perpetuated by War Department and the Air Corps. These were the issues faced by the Tuskegee Airmen during World War II. If the policy of segregation were not overthrown, the African American people on the whole would continue to face problems in all their endeavors in every field.

The Tuskegee Airmen knew these facts and so they had to overcome the demons of their so-called "Smoke Screen" experiment. The airmen went through a lot of major training that was somewhat different from that of white pilots in regards to the amounts of time spent learning about their aircrafts, which was important for all fighter pilots. Their training consisted of four levels: preflight, or ground school; primary flight training; basic military training and advanced military flight training. If the cadets successfully completed the four phases to the satisfaction of all of the instructors, they would receive their pilot wings and a commission as an officer in the

Army Air Corps. This was the situation at hand for these men and the task, being the main objective for these men, was not the only thing they had to overcome.

Even before their training begun, we saw that the airmen had to overcome the fact of being disrespected on the arrival at the Tuskegee Airfield.

"My name is aviation instructor George Spenser Roberts of class 42-C. My friends call me 'Spanky'. To you I am 'Mister Roberts'. To me you are 'Dummies'. Now. What are your names? Sound off, Dummies!"

This quote was the exact words said as an introduction to the cadet corps for the Airmen. There were no formal introductions as a way of welcoming a new group. Even though the officer was a ranking cadet, it was obvious that his words carried the notion of a lack of respect for these men.

This goes back to the issues that were faced by these airmen, considering the fact that at any other facility, white recruits were formally welcomed and treated as potential officers. Even though this particular incident was not as harsh as others, it foreshadowed many other issues to come. Some of the airmen became very stressed out because they were constantly been harassed in some form or another. These harassments were not physical but psychological instead. This was seen in a situation where all the airmen had to retake their entry exams even though they had all received grades ninety percent or better. Such factors of the issues on the airfield base, lead to failures as well as washouts. Considering that even though it was a small percentage of pilots at Tuskegee, in comparison to those of white schools, the situation did not look good for these airmen.

Of the original thirteen members of the first class of flying cadets, eight "washed out" or failed in one of the levels before basic flight training. They could not handle the psychological stress tests administered in advanced training by the military instructors.
This situation showed that things were not easy for the Tuskegee Airmen. They had to overcome their psychological stress that caused some of them to fail of dropout. This was a big issue for them and it lead to only five of the thirteen members of the first class of cadets, graduating from the training in March 1942. These five pilots received their wings and in a matter of six months, thirty -three more pilots also received their wings. The 99th Pursuit Squadron eventually had enough pilots, trained ground administrative, and medical crews to be deployed as an all-black combat unit.

Soon after, the War Department concurred with the Army Air Corps decision to send

The 99th to the North African Theater of operations.
This in itself proved that the Tuskegee Airmen had
successfully proven the experiment "Smoke Screen"
wrong. Colonel Parrish, a colonel in the Air Corps, who
saw action in WW I, gave a speech that was well received
by major newspapers and worthy of full note, gave their
farewell speech. He told the men: I must face you with
the fact that you, as Negroes, have not been particularly
encouraged to be heroic in the past. You have been more
often taught to be patient and to endure misfortune.
Those are excellent abilities and I hope you can continue
to cultivate them and keep them. But there is a time to
keep quiet and a time to fight and the time for you to fight
is soon. Not to fight for me, for the Air Corps, for
Negroes, or even for yourselves. I hope you will think of
yourselves as fighting, first of all, for this nation, not
because it is a perfect nation, and the best nation of all...I
can only remind you in the midst of these problems of
race that seem so serious now.... that we must not forget
the human race, to which we all belong, and which is the
major problem after all.... You are, first of all, all men. No
one can ask more than that you acquit yourselves like men.
Each of you, and all of us, must prove first of all that we
are capable of the dignity and nobility of manhood; that
we can when the occasion calls for it, fight and die for a

cause that is greater than any one life, or any one man, or any one group.

This was a perfect speech for the Tuskegee Airmen who received it very well. It gave them courage to continue what they were doing and it also showed how far they had come, in the process of fighting to be recognized as capable pilots.

The experiment, which was now over since the men had received their wings earlier in March, could now be looked at by those who opposed segregation, as an experiment proven wrong to high officials in the War Department and government officials who accepted "Jim Crow" as a norm in the American society. This event showed that the airmen were capable as fighter pilots and they were now ready to win a war for the nation and the common good of civilization on the whole. The Tuskegee Airmen were very happy that they would soon see action overseas.

In 1942 the airmen were deployed to North Africa, to fight the aerial war, flying in secession, P-40, P-39, P-47 and P-51 type aircraft. These gallant men still had to continue facing racism and discrimination on the home front and the battlefront. The fact that they would now face actual combat situation, meant that their struggle for recognition would not soon be over. This was the great meaning of the "Double V" philosophy, which meant that these men wanted to see victory in two places, victory at home against the segregation policies and the treatment of blacks as well as victory abroad. This was not an easy task however, and there were many issues of racial inequalities, discrimination, and riots, military and political policies that were in the way of these Airmen.

Examples of these issues on the home front was seen in places such as, Fayetteville, NC, near the Fort Bragg army post, and even in the north at Fort Dix, NJ. Events of shoot-out between Military police and black troops in these places, were somewhat common, and caused the death of men on both sides. All these events were factors that affected the Tuskegee Airmen because at that point, they were in conflicted positions. They had to prove themselves as pilots, they had to obey the regulations of the War Department with regards to segregation on the bases at home and overseas, and they had to protect themselves from any considered tyrant such as white officers who continuously tried to pick fights with them, using degrading remarks such as name calling. Even with these issues at hand, the airmen knew that their objectives of completing their bombing missions had to be met.

These objectives were the same as they had been since the farewell speech they received before leaving for North Africa. It was important to keep in mind these values of being ready to die for the common good of the civilization, while knowing that their success or failure would have an effect on the policies on civil rights, internationally as well as at home in the United States. The lists of racial issues on the home front regarding Airmen in the Air Corps continued even in the post war era when segregation policies were still in effect. One example held great significance in the changes of policies in the War Department, and the United States on the whole. The event was one that was considered unprecedented in the history of the US Army Air Force.

One hundred and one African American pilots were arrested and charged with violating the 64th Article of War, a crime that in wartime carried the death penalty upon conviction. These pilots were arrested at Freeman Field, Indiana, on April 5, 1945, because they refused to sign an order that regulated them to segregate quarters, which was a direct order from a superior officer. This all started when these officers, some of whom were combat veterans, tried to enter a segregated officers' club at Freeman Field, Indiana: "If you go in you will be put under arrest," warned the M.P. Major White approached the black officers immediately. "What is your name Lieutenant?" White addressed Lieutenant Terry. "Lieutenant Roger Terry." "What are your names," demanded White of the other two black officers. "Lieutenant Kennedy, Sir." "Flight Officer Goodman, Sir." "You are under arrest. I want you to return to your quarters," ordered White. "Why are we under arrest?" inquired Lieutenant Kennedy. "I don't have an answer to that, said Major White.

Clearly in looking at this particular issue from an international standpoint, we are able to see that White, being a major in the Air Corps, should have had answered these gentlemen as required by law, as well as the simple fact that these men were not the enemy. Perhaps this particular Major did not want them because of the policies that they as whites "in thought" had made.   We must not only look at what went on the home front because the simple fact that the Airmen were in the Corps meant that they wanted to fight with the Allied forces to defeat Hitler and the Axis forces.

Ironically, in the midst of what was a two world war for these airmen, the war in two places that goes back to the idea of the "Double-V" philosophy, not only in psychological thought, but its reality was so vivid especially because it was so well related to the international crisis of the main war. These issues will remain in history as being those that were faced by the Tuskegee Airmen in World War II. The Airmen overcame many obstacles with their superb fighting skills and their logistics in scheming out their strategic bombing missions in areas of Italy, France, and Germany. One of the missions that they did was the most dangerous because they had to escort bombers into the heart of Germany.

The high points of the month was the mission to Berlin on March 22, the bagging of three Luftwaffe jets and one possible rocket fighter, and the awarding of a Distinguished jets and one possible rocket fighter, and the awarding of a Distinguished Unit Citation, the third for the 99th. This event showed that the Tuskegee Airmen, after overcoming so many obstacles regarding their race and the "brainwashing" notion that blacks were inferior in areas of the Army Air Corps both at home and abroad, they were achieving their objective that they set out for in the first place. This was their climax and victory. They had finally gotten the opportunity to fight for the nation and attain victory.

These issues that were looked at and analyzed, proved that regardless of the racial situation during World War II, the Tuskegee Airmen fought and achieved something many did not think they would. Flying over 15, 533 sorties and 1, 578 missions throughout Europe and North Africa, The Tuskegee Airmen never lost a bomber while escorting

78

over 200 bombing missions. During this war, only 66 of these Airmen were killed and 33 became prisoners of war. In showing their achievements, we are able to see the many stages that they had to go through from the training camp in the States to actual combat abroad. On the whole, the Tuskegee Airmen courageously earned 150 Distinguished Flying Crosses, Legions of Merit and the Red Star of Yugoslavia, eight Purple Hearts, 14 Bronze Stars, 744 Air Medals and three distinguished unit citations. Their climax and victory would help the nation as well as change things for them on the home front.

It was a time for changes in the international policies relating to Civil Rights, natural laws, and international laws on the whole. The changes would help all people facing racial issues over the world. The fact that the allied forces had won the war meant that these changes would occur. Changes started to happen with the birth of the United Nation in October 1945. The UN was now in a position to confront these truths and thus affecting the policies of all unified states under the UN Charter. It is simple to look at the consequences of the achievements of the Airmen, and articulate that what they did was for the common good of society.

Others may argue that they did it as a way to rid their

situation at home in the west to become recognized by the same people who enslaved them and in which they fought to protect. Answers will always rely on history in that, the farewell speech that was given to these Airmen before their first departure abroad to fight the same war they were fighting at home; was the exact reason why they prevailed with the Allied forces. It was an international effort to save humanity from Hitler and the Axis forces.

In looking at this research from a political standpoint regarding the United States, we saw that policies were changed in the post war era by the War department. The crisis with blacks in the military and the civilian population were degrading to their conduct on the world front. Perhaps it is a question of values? This research has shown that the Tuskegee Airmen has indeed faced many trials and tribulations during World War Two. Somehow, they were able to overcome their problems while completing their missions in Europe as the first black fighter pilots in the War. Many different forms of racism were look at in that; these were the major issues that The Tuskegee Airmen had to endure. The different views by different factions of military and political officials showed the problems of the time in history, which the Airmen helped, changed. In his book, <u>A-Train-Memories of a Tuskegee Airman</u>, Lieutenant colonel, Charles W. Dryden, United States Air

Force (Retired), questioned himself and gave an answer of
how he felt about the situations faced by the Tuskegee
Airmen. The answer he gave, showed the overall outcome
of the experiences of the Tuskegee Airmen.

 Dryden wrote: "As I recall such bitter memories I cannot
help pondering some pregnant questions. For instance:
Who really is the enemy, really? Was it the Fascist abroad
or the racist at home? Was it the Germans and the North
Koreans who shot at me with intent to kill, during my two
wars? Or was it the Major general, and others like him,
who constantly waged Jim Crow warfare against African
Americans during time of peace as during times of war?
Or yet was it still others, like the Kindergarten teacher,
whose prejudice preyed on innocent children of color?"
These were some of the questions this former Tuskegee
Airman had, as he reflected on the war on a whole.

   The conclusions of his thoughts drew a relationship
between the common good that the Tuskegee airmen
fought for and the actual outcome of World War II.
Victory and the ideas of good over evil prevailed through
his views. The Tuskegee Airmen, as Americans, would
agree with Dryden when he stated: "First of all, in spite of
the many "ugly Americans" I have encountered who
savaged my spirit with bigotry, there have been a number
of "lovely Americans" who salvaged my self-esteem by

their decency". This quote shows the Tuskegee Airmen survived many trials and tribulations that went with their time in history.

As a result, World War II ended with a victory for the Allied forces and a victory for The Tuskegee Airmen who made precedence that changed the policies of the War Department and the Army Air Corps, with regards to racial discrimination and segregation, which again continued to change in the later years of the post war era with the Civil Rights movements.

The Tuskegee Airmen
Photo courtesy of: <u>Lochgarry's Blog</u>, all rights reserved.

THE WAR IS OVER

PART 5

POST WWII

We all know that the world was totally changed after the
Second World War. For one, the entire world was free
again, for the moment from tyrants like Hitler who was a
mad man. I am still quite puzzled as to why we see so
many mad men having such great power and influence of
the masses. Is it that as people of the world we are so
weak and in need of leaders good or bad? Whatever the
answer, it is not difficult to look at every country in the
world and realize that at some points there has been a mad
man at the lead of their society. Why are these people in
power? At many level we are able to see that all leaders are
controlled by a governing system and so all political leaders
could be considered puppets for the entities for which they
work. On this level it is just too difficult for the people to
have a fair say. We know that America gained a lot of
economic and national power after the end of the Second
World War. We know that this is because their soil was
never really touched other than the Japanese attack on
Pearl Harbor, which was the beginning of the major
conflicts of the war. So, America was able to help in the
process of rebuilding Europe after it was destroyed. They

sent machineries, engineers, money, and most of all made many promised many different countries relating to having a democratic society. At the time this was an ideology greatly welcomed by many nations who were seeking for a better way of life. America was the big brother model for the world and the world saw that America was striving with wealth and power and a good political structure. So it seemed. The world did not see the great chaos happening within the country. What I am talking about is the fact that the Tuskegee Airmen still had to use separate washrooms in America, and they had just won the war for the world. America was still much divided and it was not only by the races but there was also a large division between the rich and the poor. It was difficult at the time for the world to fully understand what was really going on in America who was pushing their democratic value system on the world. They did however convince many that they did in fact have a middle class in America and that is why we still now see people all around the world striving for the American way of life.

The Horowitz Paper—Recent US History since 1945

U.S. Marines of the 28th Regiment, 5th Division, raise the American flag atop Mt. Suribachi in Iwo Jima, Japan on Feb. 23, 1945. Strategically located only 660 miles from Tokyo, the Pacific island became the site of one of the bloodiest, most famous battles of World War II against Japan. (Joe Rosenthal/AP)
Photo courtesy of: **The Dallas Morning News Inc. All**

The American society in the 1950's dwelt largely with class and status. At a time when the rest of the world was recovering from the Second World War, people were trying to build the country as a model for the rest of the world to follow. These people were the capitalists who viewed America as being the world power in relation to the international economics at the time. American soil was not destroyed as in Europe and this showed the American economy at a high. In contrast, many European countries were in the process of rebuilding everything from industries, housing, and railroads that were destroyed during the war.

As the American economy flourished, people became more and more confused with regards to the distinctions of social classes. The focus on materialism intervened to replace natural values and morality of the people. The American society was suffering emotionally because of the vividness that everyone was striving to be at a certain status within the communities. This type of status was justified with materialistic possessions and Americans at the time were caught in the dilemma. Frightened by the anxieties, inferiority feeling, and straining generated by this unending process of rating and status striving, Americans were constantly trying to surround themselves with visible evidence of the superior ranking they are claiming.[1] It was clear that the visible assets that people were able to acquire, valued far greater than the emotional satisfaction one should receive from apparent success. This could show the major focus on status, which essentially allocated and separated the classes. The turn to materialism was a phenomenon, shaping people's minds into using consumer goods as a way to show status, economic class, and achievements.

Vance Packard's book, <u>The Status Seekers</u>, showed these issues in that Packard was blaming the consumer culture on capitalists who developed it. Packard knew that the situation that America was facing, found its roots through capitalists ideologies. This included the struggle for money, to be able to make more than the neighbors. America's portrayed class and status through money. The more expensive things were, the better off the person who was able to attain it would be. It was a way to relate value, money wise, to accomplishments and self-worth. In turn of this, it caused many emotional stressful lifestyles in the American society. This is what frightened the American public because there was a constant competition for the consumption of material goods as a way to gain or show status.

This was the idea of the status seekers where people were so caught in intensifying their social status, that many other problems such as race relations and the apparent class divisions were overlooked. The thought was that everything was great in America. In fact, the rest of the world should use the American prosperity as a model in the world and as way to popularize international capitalism. This was perhaps what the American economic and political sectors wanted. As it was a post war period,

America was trying to influence communist state such as the Soviet Union to conform to capitalism as a way to boost its weak economy caused by WWII. This type of economic standpoint in America contributed to the then phenomenon that the people of America were so successful, it became confusing to them, thus leaving them to find worth for their accomplishments.

Packard realized that there was a problem at a time when it seemed that none existed. The problems of materialistic consumption, as a way to show status in the classes, overlooked ethnic divisions and poverty in America. In turn of this, Packard questioned, that common among market researchers and even among those intellectuals who celebrated the results of prosperity, that sustained economic growth was turning the nation into a classless society.[2] This showed Packard recognizing that even though the economy was doing fine, such prosperity was dividing the classes even more. He realized that the increasing social mobility affected class and ethnic divisions and America was lost in its success. It was becoming the Mecca of materialism.

The average person would not be able to move up in class and status if they were not able to acquire better things than their neighbors had. In order for this to happen, the struggle for jobs in big corporations was at hand. The major groupings of the social classes were shown. The top of the hierarchy was those who held high positions in these big corporations. These people were classified as "white-collar", and others were "Blue-collar" workers. Communities and living was a big issue because it separated the classes even more. Everyone was not able to live in the same type neighborhoods because of their financial status. Some would live in big houses outside the urban community, a sign that showed they were better off. The more into the suburbs people lived, the more rich and high class they were considered to be. A "Blue-collar" worker would not be able to afford the big white house on top of the hill, out in the suburbs, unless they had inherited some money through family. A factory job alone would not bring them the material satisfaction they craved for at the time.

The idea of bigness was what the phenomenon strived off. Everything "Big" was considered better at the time. It included: big businesses, big corporations, big homes, big cars, etc. In the hierarchy of big corporation, stratification is being carried to exquisite extremes. Employees are usually expected to comport themselves in conformity with their rank, and generally do so.[3] This shows that the society was becoming more and more accepting to rank at the time. This was one of the identified conditions in American life. These issues that proved such a phenomenon, showed Americans as being materialistic animals lost in a society that was contradicting the principles that the country was founded upon.

Families were not as important as to the regards of their possessions. Their possessions were the things that alleviated them to their class and the status they had in the community. This could naturally conclude that equality in America was being lost and status reigned. The races were already facing rigid conflicts and it became clearer when the elite manifested themselves with materialism, instead of trying to unite the country and its people. America was not at all becoming a classless society as some had thought at the time. Although we still tend to think of equality as being peculiarly American and of class barriers as being peculiarly foreign, the evidence indicates that several European nations (such as Holland, England, and Denmark) have gone further than America in developing an open-class system, where the poor but talented young can use on their merits.[4] This showed that Europeans were doing a better job than America, in relation transforming a country into an open-class society. This showed that even though America was doing well economically, there was still a class division, and European countries were bringing the classes together instead of a part.

A good as the American life was at the time, Packard had identified a new condition in American life, a condition that caused problems that were not easily seen on the surface. These social issues showed ethnic groups and "Blue-collar" workers at the bottom of the food chain. This phenomenon with materialism, class, status, made things worse for everyone who was not automatically classified in the high class. Blacks, Asians, and other ethnic groups in America were not considered to be in the high class and so it would be hard for them to get the jobs in the big corporations, regardless of their qualifications. This separated the classes even more. The idea of a classless society then became more difficult to be realized.

The 1950's showed clearly a condition that Packard identified in America. It was indeed a phenomenon that focused on class and status, eliminating all other issues. The struggle for the status seekers to allocate themselves within their communities was relentless. People went through many emotional and stressful situations because of these factors. The situation at the time was a social confusion in America. People needed to make sense of what was going on and they did so with the influences of capitalism. Packard had identified a condition in America, and even his own personal story related to the phenomenon at the time.

PART 6

WHAT IS FAIR IN WAR?

During the Second World War we saw that the major Allied powers at the time had to unify for one common cause, to Stop Hitler. The three major powers of the allied forces were Britain, America, and Russia. Throughout the war we saw that all the leaders of these countries had to make many difficult decisions relating to issues the troops, social and moral issues for their countries. It was not difficult to see that Russia and its troops were the ones who played the biggest roles at specific battles, to wear out the German forces. We cannot forget the winter battles where the Russians were really prepared and laid a big blow to Hitler's troops. Along the way we saw that there were many purges from within the Russian army. The leaders at the time, Stalin, had to get rid of many of his own men as a way to secure loyalty and block any infiltrators who were working for the other. We will look at how a real general is defined in the next essay.

Stalin as a leader

Photo courtesy of: Autonomous Nonprofit Organization,
all rights reserved.

In the book, <u>The Art of War</u>, Sun-tzu describes the
qualities of a good leader. These qualities are a
determinant of whether or not a leader will be successful
in the situation of war, and give an understanding of how
the outcome of a conflict will control the destiny of their
country and its people in times of war. An Example of
such a leader can been seen in Stalin, The Soviet's military
leader in World War Two. For Sun-tzu, a good leader
should know his strengths as well as his weaknesses. This
will help them to make rational decisions in order to be
successful. One who knows the enemy and knows himself
will not be endangered in a hundred engagements. One
who does not know the enemy but knows himself will
sometimes be victorious, sometimes meet defeat. One

who knows neither the enemy nor himself will invariably be defeated in every engagement.

In looking at this statement, one must realize that these are principles that should not be overlooked. Simply, following these ideas will lead to virtual success in warfare as these fundamental knowledge and analysis of war have been tested. A general who understands these truths will be able to make the right calculations in all engagements. This also relates to the ideas of knowing when to fight and when not to fight by judging all the aspects of a situation. In knowing when to retreat and making that choice in times of battle, Sun-tzu explains that this is wise. Retreat should not be looked at as being a weakness but instead, the general who makes such a choice possesses great wisdom. This situation could be justified in an altercation when the general realizes that the enemy has the upper hand with regards to troops and military equipment as well as positioning.

It is of great benefit for a general to be wise in the sense that he or she is courageous enough to retreat, regarding the lives of his troops and the greater ultimate benefit to the outcome of war, without thinking of his own reputation. The Cliché, "living to fight another day" would be a perfect example for such a situation. Sun-tzu regarded this idea as being something every good leader should possess, essential to a good general's character. For Sun-tzu, the general encompasses wisdom, credibility, benevolence, courage, innovation flexibility and strictness. The laws for military organization and discipline include organization and regulations, the Tao of command, and the management of logistics. Those who understand them will be victorious, those who do not understand them will not be victorious.

Sun-tzu embellishes these concepts to the extent of which his theories on leadership in warfare on a whole are looked at around the world as sets of rules and regulations one must follow to be successful in war. Sun-tzu's military thoughts of a good leader could be seen through the leadership of Stalin, a Soviet leader during world war two. As a brief history, we can look at Russia's situation in world war two and analyze Stalin's abilities as a good leader in relation to Sun-tzu's test of character. Stalin did not want war against any country in World War Two. The simple fact that he even signed with Germany a non-aggression pact, shows his desires for peace between states at a time when Hitler, the leader of Germany, was so hated by many. In looking at Stalin's character, we will realize that he was in fact an honorable individual. Even though Hitler and his policies were so inhumane, Stalin still did not reject a peace pact with Germany because at that point

Germany was not considered a major threat to him. Sun-tzu would consider this a wise choice that Stalin made because he followed Sun-tzu's principles of looking at war as a last resort and thus, Stalin made a rational choice by signing agreements of peace with Hitler in order to safeguard himself from major conflicts with Germany.

At that particular time in history, we know that Hitler did not stick to his agreements with Stalin and in fact, invaded Russia as a part of his plans to take over all surrounding territories. Even though Stalin was became shocked and in fact went out of commission for a short time, he had to defend his country and its people from any attacks on them. He started this process by warning the country of their situation of war. Stalin gave a speech that even at present day could be considered one of the most influential blood sweat and tears war speech ever. The primary idea of the speech was to get everyone to unite as a whole and fight together. Stalin classified his drastic chaotic situation with the practical events of total mobilization. He got the entire country to stand behind him ready to fight.

During the process of Stalin's mobilization, many lives were lost but the people did not give up and made his army stronger. He was able to influence his people to the extent that most civilians converted into the army to serve their country.

In relating this to the ideas of Sun-tzu, Stalin could be considered clever because he was able to build one of strongest, well-equipped armies in history, and one that would eventually overcome all obstacles and defeat Hitler and Germany. Stalin went to war and succeeded because he was a good general who seemed to have mastered the ideas associated with Sun-tzu's philosophies of a good leader. This was shown through his strong counter attacks, military preparations for his defense, rational calculations, and overall knowledge of warfare. These are some of the qualities that Sun-tzu stated as requirements of a good leader, and it was clear that Stalin possessed these strengths. Furthermore, Stalin was able to organize things not only from a military standpoint but a political one as well. The Russian Government needed to stand their ground and defend themselves in order to maintain their sovereignty.

Soviet writers agreed that Stalin took a personal and direction role in the development of army equipment. Indeed, according to Zhukov, no single pattern of armament could be adopted or discarded without Stalin's approval, a measure that certainly cramped the initiative of the Commissar for defense. This showed that Stalin was confident in that he could control the process of mobilization and defeat his opponent.

    A State Defense Committee was formed to deal with
the rapid mobilization of the country's resources. As a
way to stop spies and diversionists, Stalin encouraged his
government to set up military tribunals to try anyone who
interfered with the plans. He made sure that within his
army, there was no one who would deceive him.
According to Sun-tzu, this would show a general's position
as being strict with his army. An example of Stalin's
wisdom and knowledge of warfare was also shown
through his strict process for retreat.

    Whenever any units of the Red Army were forced to
retreat, they would destroy everything behind them. They
would try to destroy the enemy by wearing them out and
making sure they did not get any valuable property such as,
fuel, grains, or any metals following Sun-tzu's words;
"Thus the wise general will concentrate on securing
provisions from the enemy. One bushel of the enemy's
foodstuffs is worth twenty of ours, one picul of fodder is
worth twenty of ours". These were the exact
considerations of Stalin's plans. He wanted to wear the
enemy out then attack when they were at their weakest
point. Stalin would wait until Hitler's troops were deep
into Russian territory and lacking resources before he
made his attack. He estimated when they were running

out of food and important military supplies such as fuel for the tanks. In relation to Sun-tzu's ideas of warfare, Stalin's strategy and tactics should have passed the test and definitely brought him victory, and this was evidenced by his ultimate victory.

For Sun-tzu, a long war is not very effective and only serves as a destroyer of resources. For him, the opportunity for an easy victory should be looked at as a quick attack where by a general should apply maximum power at the appropriate moment. This is exactly what Stalin did. He was able to make the right choice by means of rational calculations, which enabled his army to manipulate the enemy and skillfully attack them. This is how Stalin was able to show that he was a good leader. In relation to Initial Estimations, Stalin proved to be a very skillful analyst, this was just one his many strengths. These qualities in Stalin were specifically nurtured and necessary in order for him to be victorious. Indeed he was victorious and in relation to the ideologies of Sun-tzu, Stalin would pass the test of character. We are now able to see that Sun-tzu's ideologies in The Art of War, relates to that of Stalin in World War Two because he passed Sun-tzu's test of character and was victorious against Hitler of Germany. He proved himself to be a good leader and a student of Sun-tzu.

The Specter of Communism

I have spoken with many different people from many different countries about issues relating to communism versus democracy. It is a really difficult subject to discuss. When thinking in a rational sense many have said that the idea of the ideal communism would be the best for all societies. The problem is that the perfect communist state can never be truly realized because within such systems, there is still the inequality of class and status that is present. How does democracy make things better? The fact that in every system we can find good and bad points, we must always try to find a common ground. This is what a democratic society brings to the table, the reality of building a middle class to establish a balance. We will find that even when a middle class is established, there can still be many problems so we must always try to find ways to redevelop our systems such as our technology and trends. America has always been at the forefront of creating a culture, good or bad.

PART 7

THE UNITED STATES OF AMERICA VS RUSSIA

The Leffler Paper—the Cold War

Nike-Hercules missiles were designed to combat fast-moving jet aircraft flying at high altitudes. Courtesy of the U.S. Army Military History Institute.
Photo courtesy of: <u>Office of Cultural Education</u> | <u>New York State Education Department</u>.

At the end of the Second World War, The United States and Russia faced conflicts regarding their foreign policy and the standpoints of both governments. This was a critical situation where by, we saw the struggles of these two world powers. Ironically, both countries had fought together as a part of the Allied forces, against Germany and the Axis forces. It was clear however that even though these two countries had to fight together for a

better common good; they too had conflicts with the
policies of their governments.

This was a situation where we saw Russia and the
United States in constant battles over their portrayed
ideologies. On one side we had a government subjected to
the objectives of communism, one to overthrow
capitalism, and the other state, being the United States,
with their ideologies that was founded on the principles of
democracy and equality for all man. This was the base of
the conflict between the two countries. The fact that the
Allied forces had won the war, and that Russia played a
great role in the overall victory, it was not going to be easy
to conform to the suggested principles of democracy that
the United States wanted to establish in the region. We
saw that these two countries were indeed the major world
powers at the time. The United States were in a much
better situation simply because they did not have to deal
with the major issues of rebuilding the state as Russia
faced.

Both countries were making plan for major changes in
the sector of the industrialized world that was at the
forefront, a way to better their economies. The fact that
the United States had a much better economy than Russia
ever did, lead them to offer aide to Russia. This would
benefit their economy and build better relations on the

international forum, but they would have to influence Russia who was a major power at the time, to cooperate while rebuilding their country. This was not an easy thing to do however, and it goes back to the fact that in order for this to happen, Russia would have to conform to American ideologies that would eventually override the ideas of a communist state. The United States, Lansing believed, should await the formation of "a strong and stable government founded on the principles of democracy and equality of man," a government that would guarantee "every citizen of free Russia...the enjoyment of his inherent rights of life, liberty and the pursuit of happiness."[1]

This idea shows the standpoint of the United States in that; this was even before the Second World War, when Robert Lansing, American Secretary of state, opposed Bolshevism. This was the same standpoint of the United States after WWII and they were still trying to influence Russia to end their communist policies. These ideas were shown in the book, <u>The Specter of Communism,</u> where the author shows that the Cold War was inevitable. It was not a surprise to the rest of the world that after the Second World War, Stalin, the Russian leader, wanted to expand his territorial ground as well as his goal for national reconstruction. This was seen throughout some of the regions that were previously controlled by Germany, and much of the Balkan states, where Russia's power was most prominent.

In relation to the conflict between the United States, and Russia, the thought was that if Russia became too powerful on an overall scale, (the fact that they already had a powerful army, and now going after territories); they might be a threat to the world front. A threat that could easily be related to the one Hitler posed during his reign in Germany. This is why the United States wanted their political philosophy implemented in Russian foreign policy, as a way to keeping close relations in the overall process of Russian reconstruction. By offering aid to Russia, the United States would be in constant communication with them. This would happen through the process of trade and exports of goods and services. Through these processes, The United States would always know what Russia was up to, much easier than using the C.I.A to do the job. The only way for this to happen would be to convince Russia of the great opportunity they had in front of them. If Russia cooperated, the aid that they would have received from the United States would help them to rehabilitate their economy at a faster pace, while securing its share of control in Germany and Japan. This was not the case however, and this is why the Cold

War was so inevitable. Of course, Stalin's desire for cooperation had to be balanced against his other goals. He would not compromise his basic territorial demands, that is, the restoration of the 1941 borders. Nor would he forsake a sphere of influence in Eastern Europe.[2]

This is the idea that was discussed earlier in this paper where the statement that Russia would not conform easily was given. It shows that Stalin did not want to receive any aid from a western power, especially one with whom there was conflicting ideologies on politics, economics, and the social structure on the whole. The United States was considered a threat in the eyes of Stalin because of this. An important irony to look at in this situation is the fact that if Stalin had cooperated, Russia would have been much better off at the time, and perhaps even today. The question of whether or not cooperation would have prevented the Cold War is always present. Simply, we must look at history and realize that the Cold War was inevitable because of the fact that both countries, Russia and the United States, had two very different governments, which caused them to be in constant battles regarding ideologies, and governmental policies on the whole.

Leffler, the author of The Specter of Communism, shows his thoughts on the Cold War as being inevitable. Some of the factors that prove this to be true also show

the United States wanting to be the only major power.
Regardless of Russia's military strength, the United States
had a powerful new weapon, the atomic bomb. Clearly in
the analytical sense, a powerful leader would not share
information on a new powerful weapon with another
powerful leader if the notion to create a threat were non-
existing. The fact that the United States wanted to be the
only world power, and perhaps Russia felt the same way as
well, the motives of spreading American democratic
policies and the ideas of capitalism throughout Europe,
lead Harry S Truman, the American president at the time,
to try and intimidate Stalin at the Potsdam Conference in
1945. In the rational sense, one would want to keep the
fact that they had the most powerful weapon, a secret,
unless one wanted to create fear, which was exactly what
Truman did when he informed Stalin of such a destructive
weapon as the atomic bomb.

President Harry S Truman intimated the existence of a
powerful new weapon; Stalin already sensed that the
United States was hardening its position. "They want to
force us," Stalin told his associates, "to accept their plans
on questions affecting Europe and the world. Well, that's
going to happen. [3]
This quote show Stalin in a position where he feels
threatened by Truman, not only in the military sense but

also with the conflict in capitalism versus communist ideologies at the time. Stalin felt the United States should not interfere in Eastern foreign policy. Even Stalin himself knew that the war was inevitable. He expressed such a thought in his 1946 election. Stalin said that the war had arisen as "the inevitable result of the development of world economic and political forces on the basis of monopoly capitalism."[4] This shows Stalin in a position where he tried to explain the rooted causes of the Cold War. Like Leffler, Stalin brought the idea that it was not only one particular force that started the war, but also many different forces relating to politics and economics, that were powerful enough to chance a nation.

As the Cold War was inevitable, the United States took it upon themselves to play the hegemonic role on the international forum. This showed that the United States wanted to be the only world power to be reckoned with. They were trying to build the international economy, weed out communism, and protect all who conformed to these influences and relation policies that were set. This brought more and more fear to Russia, not only for its economy, but the idea of "security dilemma" was very prevalent. Perceiving threats to its security, the Kremlin tightened its grips on its satellites; seeing new signs of soviet aggression and repression, the U.S moved with alacrity to organize the rest of the world.[5] This basically shows both countries in a position of fear for each other thus, taking measures to satisfy their own policies.

In looking at the situation on the whole, I too feel that the war was inevitable. I feel that whenever there are two major powers in the world, especially those with conflicting ideologies, there likely will be a war. In understanding that such a war does not necessarily mean the utilization of military forces, we were able to see the other political and economic forces being used during the Cold War. History has proven that the common interest of states it in fact to protect their sovereignty. Regardless of conflicting ideologies, powerful states will always feel threatened by another powerful state, even if there is a balance of power. Clearly we saw that this was the happening between the United States and Russia and it proves that the Cold War was inevitable.

On the whole, we were able to recognize that the basis of the Cold War was cause by two conflicting ideologies between two major world powers. The United States sought to establish the influences of a democracy and the idea of international free trade in the post WWII period. Russia on the other hand opposed the ideas of these western objectives in the eastern sphere. Russia wanted to continue its policies of communism, while influencing other surrounding countries not to conform to the west. These conflicts eventually lead to a "security dilemma" where there two countries felt threatened by each other. Both countries utilized many counter measures as a way to protect their policies however the war was inevitable. This shows some of the major happenings in the world after the Second World War. Leffler, the author of: The Specter of Communism tries to give his readers a better understanding of what the Cold War was all about. The ideas of many different forces other than military force were looked at in an overall spectrum relating to the obstacles of threat for both sides. Leffler illustrated the ideological differences between the United States and Russia and it was a way to look at history and better understand two great powers in the Post WWII era.

American Liberalism and Lyndon B. Johnson

Lyndon Baines Johnson was the thirty-sixth US

President (1963-69) and the first President elected from a Southern state since before the Civil War. He succeeded to the presidency after the assassination of John Kennedy on November 22, 1963.

After the assassination of JFK, the incoming president needed to really work hard to try and cover some bases that the previous president wanted to touch. This was the issue of the races. The racial policies in America at the time needed to be changed. There were problems on both side from the racist whites who did not think equality was a good thing, and the blacks who used violence as a way to achieve equality. Both were wrong and so political entities needed to lay the groundwork for a better America. We will see that the issues were severe and Lyndon B. Johnson delivered the federal government from losing all black who at the time did not have faith in politics or the federal government on the whole.

The American society in the 1960's went through many changes under the leadership of President Lyndon B. Johnson. These changes sought make a difference to better the entire structure of the American political, economic, and social life. From the book, <u>Lyndon B. Johnson and American Liberalism,</u> Bruce Schulman writes that Lyndon B. Johnson "embodied the contradictions of political liberalism...orchestrated its triumphs, and endured its agonies." [1] As a way to better understand this statement, a brief explanation of the time should be looked at. It was during the Cold War period where America seemed to be prospering from its economic democratic standpoints in contrast to the rest of the world. They made a model for the rest of the world to follow. They fought against communism while influencing the rest of the world to join the race for world capitalism, for open markets and free trade that was good for the world economy.

America seemed to have been doing great on the world front however; many domestic issues plagued the country. These issues had to do with the great injustices in America at the time. African Americans, elderly people, children, education, tax, and unemployment were at the forefront of these problems facing the American people. Race relation conflicts were at a high. Elderly people were not getting justice with regards to the treatment they were getting after dedicating their lives to building America and having to fight for social security. Taxes were at a high and were not in favor to the less fortunate. The education system faced many problems with its conditions, not being able to cater to all children regardless of race or color. The unemployment rate was at a high and it caused much social unrest.

The statement made by Schulman was important for many reasons. It told the reader that in the midst of all these happenings, someone stood up for the common good of the American people. Simply, at such a time in history it was rear to see an individual in the political sector that did not conform to the political, social, and economic policies at the time. The society was not at a balance in these aspects. Lyndon B. Johnson wanted to change these ideals and make America a better place to live for all people. The thought of this was the "Great society", a place that would give people of all backgrounds a chance to succeed in America.

Lyndon B. Johnson was a leader who recognized that rapid changes needed to be made in America. This would be the only way that his envisioned society would become a reality. The forefront of these changes was based on making social policies that would make the social atmosphere better. He needed to start with the Civil Rights policies, not only because rapid changes were required, but also it was a continuation on the policy of the late John F. Kennedy. Under the leadership of LBJ these policies would see light. Schulman's quote intended to prove this to its readers. To show them that LBJ recognized the major issues, adjusted to making changes, endured all negative obstacles, and implemented the law as he saw fit. He defied the contradictions to political liberalism at the time. The contradictions that he wanted to set aside were basically summed up in one of his addresses.

At his address before a joint session of the congress on November 27, 1963, LBJ made an important statement. This statement summarized the contradictions. Johnson stated: " so let us put an end to the teaching and preaching of hate and evil and violence. Let us turn away from the fanatics of the far left and the far right, from the apostles of bitterness and bigotry, from those defiant of law, and those who pour venom into our nation's bloodstream."[2] Here Johnson defied all Americans who would be against his policies. These were the Southern white racists who supported the segregation movement. Black Americans who used radicalism as means to achieve equality. White mobs that continued to violate the human rights laws and natural laws, by taking the law into their own hands and doing many illegal killings. LBJ knew that the great society could not be achieved if these tyrants existed in the society.

Liberalism and its ideological principles of liberty and freedom for all were fresh in the suggested and implemented changes made by LBJ and his constituents. The fact that he was able to challenge congress and make positive changes in political and social policies showed that liberalism succeeded. He waged a war against poverty throughout America and caught the attention of many Americans who were at a stalemate thinking that the federal government did not care about the common people and their common problems. LBJ, through his leadership and demands showed the entire nation that he would make the difference in order to achieve a great society. In 1966 at a White House conference on civil rights, LBJ stated: "in stripping away legal barriers-in opening political opportunity-in attacking the lack of skills and jobs, and education and housing that are really the taproots of poverty. In all these efforts we have made mistakes," LBJ conceded. " But I came here tonight- at the end of a long day-to tell you we are moving and we shall not turn back."[3] LBJ showed congress that he was determined to fight for the rights of all who faced injustices in America. He recognized that even though his push would perhaps even cause war in the American streets, he needed to implement these changes because it was the only way for success.

Liberalism was a success. Its concepts went hand in hand with LBJ leadership. His push for the civil rights act and voting rights laws were just a few of the things that showed his leadership, while complementing the principles of liberalism. Practical and theoretically actions were taken. These actions showed LBJ defying the contradictions of political liberalism. The success of his policies showed that liberalism had indeed succeeded and his leadership also played an important role. LBJ and his constituents sought to challenge congress into making chances to accommodate the vision of a great society and they accomplished it. No other president had ever achieved what LBJ did. Many of his predecessors had tried but none were able to see the actual implementations on the suggested policies carried out. This shows that both liberalism and LBJ's leadership had succeeded.

Black Americans were given hope, the education system would flourish, and the unemployment rate would drop all because of the leadership of LBJ and his constituents. The struggle was still not over however and all this success gave a damper to LBJ politically, because at this point many white southerners were still dead against the move to achieve equality and prosperity for all. This was the agony the LBJ had to endure, in reference Schulman's quote. LBJ was losing many supporters in the south because of his rapid demand for equality. This was a stand that no other president had taken before. This standpoint came as a surprised to many Black Americans who had lost faith in the federal government. It also surprised many white southerners who thought the demands for rapid changes were the wrong things to do. LBJ regarded this as a contradiction to his policies and this was earlier expressed through a special message to congress in March 1965.

He expressed that rights must be opportunities. This was at the forefront of his policies. He spoke out that all Americans should have the privileges of citizenship no matter what race they were. He wanted all to see that everyone had the right to vote and that his policies would see that it became a reality. LBJ stated: "I would like to caution you and remind you that to exercise these privileges takes much more than just legal rights. It requires a trained mind and a healthy body. It requires a decent home, and a chance to find a job, and the opportunity to escape from the clutches of poverty."[4] LBJ wanted to make it clear to the American people that he was going to adjust his government for a better society. This was the idea of his liberalism that succeeded. It succeeded because the bills that were suggested to congress were eventually passed and gave blacks and whites alike the opportunity to achieve success in America. LBJ had also succeeded because he became the first to suggest and implement policies that had never been fully acted upon by the federal government before. This showed that his leadership as well as his ideas of liberalism worked together. His vision of a great society was actually in the making. He was able to set a foundation that would chance the political, social, and economic systems in America forever.

For the first time in history changes were being made to support all Americans regardless of their race of financial background. At a White House conference in 1966 Johnson made another powerful statement that showed his leadership and foreshadowed the success of liberalism. He concluded that: " we shall either move this nation towards civil peace and towards social justice for all of its citizens, or for none."[5] Here Johnson showed that he was truly a leader. He showed that he would not conform and bow to the politics of the past. This statement would solidify his plans that he and his constituents would fight for. This was a way to achieve the great society with freedom and justice for all. In the attempt to implement his policies, LBJ showed his leadership and his ideas of American liberalism.

History was indeed in the making. For the first time in American history, Black Americans were given the opportunity to hold official positions in the government.

By making federal employment available to blacks, LBJ
was able to change the economic conditions for many
blacks in America. With his leadership the federal
government was finally taking and stance through positive
action. Slowly but surely blacks were in a position where
they would be recognized, treated equally, while having the
same privileges as whites. Many problems were still at
hand but these changes showed a great start towards a
great society.

Lyndon B. Johnson " Embodied the contradictions of
political liberalism…. orchestrated its triumphs, and
endured its agonies. He did this through his leadership
and his constant agitation of congress to support his
policies. He succeeded by sticking to the fundamental
principles of liberalism and not giving up when things
became difficult. Fundamentally, Johnson wanted to
change the entire structure of American life and he did. It
was not easy and obstacles such as the many riots that
took place while he was trying to get his policies
implemented were some of the agonies he had to endure.
The fact that he did not give up with congress showed that
he orchestrated the triumphs of his liberation push in
America. This standpoint was historic in the history of
American politics. Lyndon B. Johnson showed the nation
that the idea of a great society was not just a vision. He

made it a reality.

The Civil Rights Movement

When we think of the Civil Rights Movement, most people automatically focus on Martin Luther King, or Malcolm X. These were the brave heroes who fought for equal rights and justice for blacks in America in the sixties. They were known for their different approaches for bringing about these changes. King used the philosophy of non-violence, which was deeply associated with the teaching of Gandhi, while X; use the approach that incorporated violence as self-defense especially in times of protest. Regardless of the two very different approaches, the two men really complimented each other. Many would agree that they needed each other at the time.

The Wright Paper

In the book, <u>Uncle Tom's children</u>, Wright's accounts in his different stories showed his fiction as being that of protest literature. As a way to make sense of this type of writing, Wright's messages through his stories gave many foundational solutions for blacks to never give up the endeavors for self-actualization and empowerment. The writings are that of Negro fiction that sought to give readers an interpretation of the constant tragic of the Negro life in America at the time. In relation to the ideologies of Jim Crow, Wright wanted to show his readers that blacks were being oppressed by the system.

Wright was able to recognize the major problems facing African-Americans. These problems were associated with the fact that he used his writing to protest against them. In an undermining way he also suggested ways to respond to the problems that blacks were facing. Each character in his story played a certain part that was important to the messages and the picture Wright was trying to paint in the readers mind. The fact that the book was intended specifically for blacks, white readers also read his book and the apparent protest was acknowledged by mainstream America. Wright wanted to do something that no other black writer had done before. With his writing, he did not want to cater only for the white population as he thought others have done in the past. Instead, his writing would touch and influence black America to think and act on the great injustices they were facing. The literature told stories about the different situations blacks would face and the idea of segregation, a system that was known as Jim Crow. Wright wanted to lash out against Jim Crow, a system that was prevalent at the time and one that he grew up in. He wrote about the injustices Jim Crow brought and this is why his writing gives the feeling of protest.

Wright resisted the idea of becoming complacent with what he viewed as "the attempt by whites to break the spirits of Southern blacks, to make them complicities in their own oppression".1 The idea here was that he felt blacks were so brain washed that they sometimes settled with being looked at as inferior to whites. Wright felt that his people have been oppressed for too long, that the ideology of Jim Crow was a way of holding blacks down and keeping them down. The system would continue to influence and brainwash African-Americans into thinking they could never achieve equality with the white man, thus settling for inferiority.

Wright saw this idea of the white man wanting to inflict a major systematic power of oppression by means of the segregation system at the time, as the "key racist imperative". This was the biggest issue that blacks had to overcome. He sought to resist this racial standpoint as much as he could by turning to reading and forms of creative. This was a way for him to build himself, a way to gain knowledge and wisdom. After relating what he was reading to the idea of expressing himself and the level of free expression that writing brought, he ventured into forming his own concepts of things. This was perhaps the beginning of his venture into protest literature whereby he wrote about the grave injustices faced by African-Americans in a Jim Crow system. At this point in his life Wright knew he needed to go out on his own to seek a life away from the south where he lived. As the introduction of Uncle Tom's Children stated, " for a young black man in the south with such as rebellious attitude, there were few viable options; flight was ultimately the one that Wright took".2 This showed young Wright at a point in his life where he felt he had to leave the south for his journey of experiencing other places in America that could be better for him and his family. In the process Wright experienced many ups and downs while trying to make a better life for himself. Being a black man in America at the time meant that he would have to carry with him all the burden of his people regardless of where he was. These experiences carved a solid mold into his mind as perhaps the greatest influence for him to protest through his writing. He saw the injustices of the unbalanced socio-economic situation facing his people and the fact that society seemed to have been against him.

Wright was reading a lot at this point, especially writings that he could relate to and which empowered him with the ideas of self-expression. From one of the books he read, he was very impressed with the way the author was able to articulate his words and overall writing style, attracting Wright into wanting to write and express himself in the same manner. He felt that perhaps as a writer he could use words as a weapon and lash out on America for oppressing his people. For him, writing was a safe domain where he was able to express his feelings and emotions on behalf of his people. This was shown early on in Wright's life when, he became intrigued by others whose writing influenced him to express himself through protest literature. He thought, "could words be a weapon? Well yes, for here they were (in reference to what he had read). Then maybe, perhaps, I could use them as a weapon?"3 Young Wright was building himself and forming theories about social context in America so he could write and protest about them through fiction. He was indeed setting the stage for becoming one of the most prominent black writers who wrote protest literature.

It was very obvious that Wright wanted to resist the so-called "key racist imperative". He showed this in one of his stories where he presented his mother as being one who was not able to resist the oppression. He showed the situation with his mother as being complicities in her own oppression. He considered her to be so caught up into believing that white folks were superior that he knew he had to make a change. The story was about him and his black friends who play war games using cinders as weapons. On one particular day however, a gang of white boys became involved in the war games. This event leads to the use of broken bottles by the white boys, which lead to a bottle cutting Wright behind the ear while trying to escape.

In relation to what Wright regarded was an attempt by whites to further oppress blacks, this story was a prime example because he showed the actions of his mother as catering to the ideals of whites that he intended to resist. He explained that even though he was not in the wrong for playing war games, as he had always played war with his friends, he received a beating like no other. The incident with the white boys should have never happened; he should never play games with the white boys again. This was the mentality of his mother who did not see or realize the young boys sometimes play rough and the incident could have happened even without the presence of the white boys. Regardless, Wright's mother gave him a serious scolding for playing war games and getting hurt by white boys who came from across the tracks. " She would smack my rump with the stave, and, while the skin was still smarting, impart to me gems of Jim Crow wisdom"4 Wright explained that his mother scolded him even though he was not at fault for what had happened. It showed that because whites were involved, automatically, lead to Wright being in the wrong because he had no right for playing with them in the first place. This was the idea of the Jim Crow influence that had impoverished the minds of blacks into thinking white were a superior race.

Wright wanted to see change for his people. This is why his fictions were clearly protest literature. If he were able to stir up any controversy among the American populace, then his words would be a weapon, a weapon in the battle for changing injustices for blacks in America. By protesting with words, eventually they will bring by changes as long as the American mainstream was reading. He sought that his people should take a stand, a stand that was perhaps one of the major solutions that he suggested. This type of standpoint was seen in his story, <u>Bright and Morning Star</u>. This story gave the reader the depicted ideas that Wright was trying to portray as being the fundamental solution for blacks at the time. They needed to stop acting on behalf of the Jim Crow mentality, actualize themselves, and never give up the struggle for black empowerment.

The story showed a mother and her son bound to bring changes for blacks in the region they were living. After enduring many trials and tribulations that the whites had to offer, the mother swore she would protect her son and his comrades who were communist. At such a time, the communist party in America was the only party advocating issues of human rights, justice and equality for the unfortunate people in America. Many blacks joined the party because of this fact, in hope that perhaps changes would come by faster for African- Americans. The solution would be that blacks should never give up the struggle. If they kept the faith the naturally better things would come. Wright wrote about how the locals found out about a black revolution soon to take place. An important meeting was to be held and Whites did not want it to happen.

Eventually there was a traitor in the group who wanted to bring them in to justice. This particular traitor tricked the mother whose son was one of the official members of the party. This lead to both mother and son being killed in the end however, the white official and his mob did not get the names of the comrades who they were in search of. Both mother and son died for a common good, to protect a group they felt would help blacks reach their goal of self-determination. "she felt the heat of her own blood warming her cold, wet back. She yearned suddenly to talk. "yuh didn't git whut yut wanted! N yuh ain gonna nevah git it!"5 This was at the end of the story where Wright showed a mother and her son staying loyal to something their race depended upon. They died believing in something, believing that blacks would see better days after this particular meeting that was to be held, a sacrifice as Jesus had done for man.

The task of constructing new traditions and new wisdom was one a difficult one. Wright wrote these stories to express the injustices with hope that America will come to such realization as well. The characters in Bright and Morning Star, showed that they would no longer conform the "the age-old repression formed under slavery and peonage" a term used by Sociologist, Allison Davis. In relation to <u>Uncle Tom's children,</u> these accounts were prime examples that Wright used in his writing to reject the past and its Jim Crow ideologies that was inflicted upon blacks.

Wright's fictions were clearly protest literature and he sought solutions through his writings. From the book, <u>Uncle Tom's Children,</u> Wright depicted the major problems facing African-Americans as being the struggle to alleviate themselves from their oppression caused by slavery and Jim Crow. Through his writings he sought to use his words as weapons, to agitate America as a way of bringing changes. On the whole, the major message that was spoken to blacks through Wright's writing was the idea that they should never give up hope.

Richard Wright was born September 4, 1908 in Roxie, Mississippi.

The Dubois Paper

In the early 20th century, the American society faced many serious problems with regards to the color line and segregation that was prominent at the time. At such a time in history, there was not a great deal of blacks that were considered scholarly writers, able to influence the nation as well as the rest of the world, through writing. This is where W.E.B Du Bois, a writer, historian, comes into play. Du Bois wrote about <u>The Souls of Black Folks,</u> in the various essays. These essays sought to explain the writer's thoughts and outlook regarding blacks in America in relation to the many obstacles they faced. As freedmen, it was obvious at the time that blacks still did not get treated equally and in trying to find meaning, influence changes, and greater understanding of the issues of the color line in America, Du Bois wrote about it.

His essays were very well written in that; it created a great deal of controversy from those that analyzed and

interpreted it. Like everything that we do as people, we do
not always agree with each other. Du Bois messages, in his
essays, were powerful enough to influence people into
thinking about the races. The issues they both faced in
America, at a time in history where ideas of
industrialization and capitalism, classes and status were at
the forefront, that which was perhaps the most important
objectives for the political and economic sectors in
America. There was no doubt however that the problem
of the races existed in the midst of it all, and it was causing
many conflicts within the communities throughout the
United States. Many letters were written to Du Bois about
the Souls of Black folks. These were letters from many of
the most highly educated people, black and white, at the
time. On the whole, these essays could be considered very
influential because it said to black America, that they
should actualize themselves and make sense of the many
changes and continue the process for attaining a better life
in America. As well as recognizing one's self as an entity
in the American social life at the time, much needed to be
done. In contrast, it was telling whites that the problems
between the races were serious and should be dwelt with.
America should not hide from these ideas as a way of
trying to forget slavery ever happened. The thought of
where they (as blacks) stood in society with regards to

society's standards needed to be addressed because there was a lack of equality between races. Those who were educated such as Du Bois gathered and shared ideas as a way to better the race and set a foundation for changes in America.

In trying to look at both sides and measure the main depicted conflicts, it was clear that blacks and whites alike, face many of the same problems especially in the labor sector, where there was an upper and lower class. The classes were distinguished through the jobs that each individual held and in relation to DuBois's explanation of issues affecting communities, blacks and whites faced the same issues as poor laborers. This idea was touched on by one of the people who wrote to Du Bois and criticized him for overlooking the relation of the colored man to the labor problem. "You do not seem to be aware that the white laborers of the North are facing the same alternative of starvation, or submission and unceasing, unrecompensed toil."[1] This was a way of explaining to Du Bois that these problems were not only of the south but of the north as well. This basically showed the thoughts of a Northerner who wanted Du Bois to focus more on the conflict between capital and labor in America on a whole. It showed whites in the labor force were facing the same injustices as blacks. This could be looked at as some of the problems affecting both communities and the intellectuals at the time knew it, while then peasants did all that was required.

As a way to try and solve the problems of the color line, these are some of the things we must look at. Both blacks and whites are able to relate to as experiences that may bring the races closer together. Experiences within the classes were included in some of Du Bois's depictions, as a way of looking at the history of blacks. In relation to shared experiences there were many whites in the south that were facing poverty, while been looked at by their own people as being trash because of their class and economic status that could be closely related to the poor blacks in the region. Du Bois, being black and knowledgeable about the problems of the color line, he spoke out on the happenings with blacks whereby; the dominant force that was able to mend his thoughts together included the spiritual world for his people. Through all the tails of sorrow and revealing sadness, it gave worth for a better life for blacks. This idea of spirituality in blacks may perhaps even foreshadow the optimistic outcomes of the objectives that were set forth in the minds of many who sided with Du Bois and what he stood for. The idea that one-day blacks and whites alike would be able to live together in unity, understanding that we are all a creation of God with shared experiences as a way to put the pieces of the puzzle together.

One of the letters that Du Bois had received in criticism to his writings in <u>The Souls of Black Folks</u> came from a William James, a professor who had been a mentor and a teacher to DuBois, while he was studying at Harvard. In the letter, Mr. James explains to DuBois that Souls is too despairing, arguing that he was not wedded to the "minor key". The thought as it could be interpreted, was that Du Bois's writing showed no hope for the "minor key" that were the blacks in America. In continuation Mr. James explained that he was not wedded to the "minor key", which basically meant that Du Bois should not waste his time in trying to bring by changes in America for blacks, because they were hopeless. This was in part a psychological thing for blacks at the time. The question of Mr. James's standpoint on race relations may draw a conclusion to his initial criticism of Du Bois's work. In knowing that Du Bois was in a position where he was able to influence America through his writing may have led to the criticism of his work being too despairing.

Many answers could be drawn from these questions and it would still remain that Du Bois was a black man who wanted to see a better life for his people. Regardless of how others would stare him he felt obligated to express his ideas in hope for later changes. This was shown in Du Bois's response to Mr. James, where he concluded: You must not think I am personally wedded to the "minor key" business-on the contrary I am tuned to a most aggressive & unquenchable hopelessness. I wanted in this case simply to reveal fully the other side to the world.[2]

This basically showed Du Bois in defense that even though he is not personally responsible for changing American ideologies of blacks, he was at the forefront of their experiences and thus, he had to write about these happenings. Obviously, being a black man that time; he would have wanted to see his people in a better position than they were at the time. The problems did not only deal with segregation but it dwelt with problems of equality across the board.

Blacks had nothing to show for all the hundreds of years that the white man enslaved them. They lived in the worst conditions both socially and economically. Even though they were free they were still oppressed in the mind. They had to settle for worst jobs, or even stay and work with their old masters mainly because there were not many choices for them. They did not have the opportunity as Du Bois had to become well educated as a way to better themselves. This is why Du Bois stresses the

idea of education that blacks were lacking and that
government should provide adequate funding to foster a
better education for blacks. A people thus handicapped
ought not to be asked to race with the world, but rather
allowed to give all its time and thought to its own social
problems.[3] This showed clearly that blacks had some
social problems whereby the lack of education was a
critical one. The fact that Du Bois recognized this through
his writings could prove that there was in fact hope.
Blacks needed to uplift themselves and
Du Bois's writing was essential to this entire process.
These are the reasons for hope as DuBois sees it.

Reasons for hope were the battle cry. Du Bois's essays
showed these aspects of the human social life as a
relentless quest to gain identity within a culture. Away with
the black man's ballot, by force or fraud,-and behold the
suicide of a race. Nevertheless, out of the evil came
something of good,-the more careful adjustment of
education to real life, the clearer perception of the
Negroes' social responsibilities, and the sobering
realization of the meaning of progress.[4] The lack of
resources was a reality of the education problems for
blacks and this realization gave them hope. As a people,
they knew what they had to do in order to achieve an
identity and progress as a culture. This shows that Du

138

Bois's writing is ultimately encouraging and inspirational, proving wrong Mr. James critique of <u>The Souls of Black Folks</u>. Surely then, it is possible to deal with such deeply in grained problems such as the color line in the early 20th century. The process of doing so starts in the recognition of a problem, which is ultimately realistic and optimistic as a way to bring changes. This is why Du Bois wrote about the various experiences of blacks. As a black intellect, Du Bois knew he had to write about these things. That is why he responded to Mr. James in the manner he did. In realizing that he was not bound to solving the problem of the color line in its entirety, he still wanted to reveal to the world the American tragic for blacks in the society at such time in history.

The optimistic idea laid the story of hope for a people. As being a part of society, naturally everyone needs hope in life. In those days the churches were very important and they gave hope to blacks in America. This building is a central clubhouse of a community of a thousand or more Negroes. Various organizations meet here,-the church proper, the Sunday-school, two or three insurance societies, woman's societies, secret societies, and mass meetings of various kinds.[5] The church was regarded highly as a spiritually safe ground for blacks to commune. Here they could exchange charity and strengthen their lives. It is explained that the church was not only used as a religious center, but it was also a social, intellectual, and economic center. This gave reasons for hope. The ideas that blacks are very spiritual, and the ideologies of the church as a real conserver of morals, could actualize a final conclusion that the situation being a good one at the time for blacks because it was a positive starting point. The church gave them hope, and these reasons lead the relentless struggle for a better life.

Throughout the essay, the focus on Du Bois writing was looked at. In the intentions to prove ultimately that his writing of The Souls of Black Folks was not despairing as one of his critiques, Mr. William James, had claimed it to be. The writing in itself recognized the songs of sorrow, redemption, and prosperity that soared as reason for hope. This way the realistic and optimistic way the problem of the color line could have been dwelt with at the time. The Souls of Black Folks, was essential to that because it was able to capture the minds of many intellectuals' blacks and whites alike.

W.E.B Du Bois

Photo courtesy of: BlackPast.org.

PART 8

INTERNATIONAL CRIME

When you think of international crimes happening around
the world today what is the first thing that comes to your
mind? For me, the first thing that comes to my mind is the
fact that the world powers should do something about it.
Whatever the issue might be they should do something
about it to help the people of the world to live better lives
like us. Is that not what should happen? Obviously, but
as you might know these things are never so easy and this
is why as I stated in the beginning, we see that the UN is
not as powerful as many might think. The problem is that
the members of the UN are supposed to protect the
people of the world but they don't. We are able to see this
every day. Is the not a crime against the world powers,
when they allow atrocities to happen in the world and do
nothing about it? I came to the conclusion that these
powerful states only help countries when they have an
interest in such region. At the end of the day it is quite
simple to see that these interests are associated with
money, territories and resources. We somehow however,

forget the most important resource, the people of the
world who all deserve to live a life of security and
happiness. We all must die. So, why can't we all share in
the happiness of life and living?

US Foreign Policy and Genocide in Rwanda

**'The civil war in Rwanda and the ethnic massacres
were an integral part of US foreign policy, carefully
staged in accordance with precise strategic and
economic objectives.'**

When looking at political issues in war and peace, we are able to see that the issue of Genocide is a very serious crime that has occurred during times of peace and times of war. A state that tries to use its political power to commit such a crime discredits itself against the doctrines of human rights, international law, natural laws, and all the principles therein. The United Nation carries the responsibility of dealing with the issues of genocide in that, it is considered an international crime. The consequences of genocide may bring the many questions to the table, questions dealing with the principles of morality and natural laws on a whole. In essence, states that belong to the United Nations should try to support the laws that are associated with genocide being that it is an international crime. Whenever a state commits the crime of Genocide, states that belong to the United Nations (United States) should intervene and use the necessary measures to prevent and punish the crime. If such a state chooses not to intervene it may become weak in the sense that they become the prey to the state that has committed the crime.

These political issues have been going on throughout history and we are able make analysis and interpretations of the different questions that have dwelt with these issues.

Many philosophers, political officials, and writers have written about the issues dealing with questions such as, what a state should do in the event that a conflict against their policies arises. What consequences may occur from their decisions?

These are the issues and questions that arise from looking at a quote written by Machiavelli, the renowned philosopher. These questions may be answered with an analysis of the specific quote, while relating the interpreted thought to the international crime of Genocide, and how the United States have dwelt with the problem of Genocide that happened in Rwanda, Africa. This quote that will try to explain what happens when a state does not intervene, taken from the book, The Prince, Machiavelli sought to establish a state capable of resisting foreign attack. He describes a method by which a prince can acquire and maintain political power.

This was a time in history where beliefs were very important and Machiavelli's belief was that rules should not be bound by traditional ethical norms. This meant that rules might be discovered by deduction from the political practices of the time as well as from those of earlier periods. Machiavelli stated in Prince:

If you do not intervene, you will remain the prey of the

victor.…. Princes who lack resolution take the path of
neutralization in order to avoid a present danger and for
the most part find it the path to ruin.

This quote was written in the 1500th and relates to some
political decisions that states must make in modern day
politics. In those days, the prince had to make the choices
of the necessary steps to take with certain political issues
of the time.

With regards to interventions and princes relating to
states, Machiavelli felt that if a state does not intervene, it
would remain the prey to the state that is committing a
crime such as genocide.

In this event, a state (A) who chooses to stay neutral
whenever there is a conflict that should involve them, in
order to maintain their present power or prevent loss of
power, lacks accommodation for its policies that may lead
to state (A) becoming weak while destroying a state (B)
who has become the victim from the lack on intervention.
Is it a weakness with the morality of that state? Many
political philosophers may agree that these decisions do
carry principles that are a direct influence from the norms
of a society and ideas of morality. Morality however, may
be also looked at as a back burner in comparison to
"interest of state" that state uphold as being first priority in

all their political endeavors and decisions.

In relation to a modern day situation that involves states and intervention, examples could be seen from Rwanda, where genocide took place, and the United states who did not intervene. Regarding Machiavelli's quote, this situation is an example of the many political issues that has been going on throughout history. The facts are the United States has been legally obligated to stop crimes of genocide since the end of the Reagan era in America. This is where we can also question the standpoint of the United Nations for not having an enforcement mechanism to carry out on the international front, the objectives of their commitment to the 1948 convention on the prevention and punishment of the crime of genocide. In an advertisement from the Citizens for Action Inc., this statement taken from the New Republic said: 1994 Rwanda.

President Clinton, after being told of the ongoing genocide (over 800,000 men, women and children murdered in 47 days), refuses to intervene to stop the attempted extermination of the Tutsis because of United States' priorities (national strategic interest). This shows clearly that the United States did not care to help Rwanda because there would be no benefit in doing so. From the standpoint of the United States, benefits would involve its economic, political, or military interest. This would involve raw materials, goods and services; types of trade relation that was not established between the two countries and thus, the United States felt that they did not need to help Rwanda.

Others may disagree with these thoughts simply because interventions may lead to more conflict in any situation. It is difficult to know when U.S. efforts might have been decisive had they simply been more sustained of better orchestrated. While some of Washington's missteps have clearly been idiotic, other bad decisions are harder to fault.

This basically shows that at times, the United States become conflicted with the political decisions that they must make and sometimes they make the wrong choices. This relates to their situation with Rwanda in that, the United States chose not to intervene. The non-intervention however, caused many lives that might have been prevented if the U.S had deployed troops into Rwanda. These are the situations that States face with regards to making decisions of interventions. In relation to Machiavelli's quote, we are able to realize that because the United States did not intervene, thousands of lives were lost and Rwanda became the path that was ruin.

On the whole, we should consider that this situation is perhaps one that has been around for a very long time. When dealing with genocide, we saw this in the earlier years during World War Two where President Roosevelt, refused to intervene to stop the extermination of the Jews in the death camps, again it was because of the Allies priorities of the nation's strategic interest. It is then obvious to realize that the issues dealing with racial, cultural, religious, ethnic groups, are that of lower politics and is not considered as important to states. High politics is much more important, and the national interest of states are included in high politics.

The situation of WWII and the modern situation of genocide in Rwanda show the ethnic groups that were being killed. In Germany, it was the Jews and in Rwanda, it was the Tutsi, being killed by another ethnic group, the Hutus. In both situations we saw that a state that had the power to stop these killings did not do so because the situation did not involve high politics. Ethnic groups and their political issues are dwelt with in lower politics in powerful states that consider other objectives in high politics as being more important. This was the situation in Rwanda. The United States did not consider the killings of thousands of Rwandans as being in the national strategic interest. Rwanda had nothing to offer, they were not a world power, and they have no relations with the U.S. With this in mind, we still must not forget that the United States is a part of the United Nations. The fundamental principles of the UN should have been sufficed for the U.S. to intervene even though they are obligated to do so. This may bring about many questions because the UN should have intervened much earlier that they did.

Many would say that the UN and the U.S is at fault for what happened in Rwanda in 1994. The fact of the matter is that Genocide is an international crime and thus, the world community should be held at fault for what happened. Many other states could have intervened in Rwanda by deploying troops. It all boils down to the fact that states care about their interest only, in the event that they are able to play neutrality whenever conflicts arise in other states, they do so to protect themselves and maintain their power. This was the situation with the U.S. and Rwanda.

PART 9

A DISCUSSION—THE *FIVE MOST IMPORTANT EVENTS OF THE ORIGINS OF WWII*

Hitler's withdrawal from the disarmament conference and The League of Nations (October 1933)

Withdrawal from the Conference for the Reduction and Limitation of Armaments and the League of Nations, 1933

As an international issue, disarmament was not fully accepted by Hitler and his army. The western powers such as France and Britain, did not want to give Germany the power of equality in armaments. This event leads to Hitler's secret actions to accelerate rearmaments. The public did not realize what Hitler was doing because he continued to preach his love for peace while making proposals for disarmaments. I think this was a critical moment in the history of that time because the public was being lied to, and Hitler had his own agenda to try and take over the world.

The relationship between Germany and the Soviet Union (January 1934)

German and Soviet troops shaking hands following the <u>invasion of Poland</u> in September 1939.

The German-Soviet relations were deteriorating very fast in a time when bilateral agreements were so important to

Hitler. The fact that Hitler wanted to reduce tensions on the Eastern front leads to his agreements with Poland, even though he had planned to destroy them. Once again, he was just looking out for his own interest. The non-aggression pact was just meant to stall things in order for him to buy time to build up his army. This was significant because at the time, the Soviet Union joined The League of Nations and Started to pursue their own plans for peace in agreements with France. Hitler did not like that at all and major tension grew between both countries.

Hitler admitting to rearmaments (April 1935)

Adolf Hitler: Rearmament and new alliances

This was a situation when Hitler officially admitted his secrets of rearming. Other powers such as in Britain, France, and Italy, were very much against German actions. This was important because it showed that Hitler was asking for a fight. The three countries formed a united front in combination with The League of Nations, and sanctions were made against Germany. Germany's isolation from the rest of the European countries that embraced the coalition was just a way for Hitler to feel that his actions would be justifiable. The Soviet Union for example, entered in alliance with Czechoslovakia that same year, while also making agreements with France. Hitler now knew that the masses were against him and that only pushed him to try and expand his territory.

The Great Depression (Early 1930s)

The Great Depression in the 1930s began with the
stock market crash on October 24, 1929.

The great Depression that was faced by the world in the
early nineteen thirties created many unrest conflicts
between countries. These conflicts related to trade

settlements, peace, and many other treaties.

Countries wanted to begin the process of progress in order to rebuild their social, economic, and political status in the world. This was a way for countries to feel secure and thus, important. Many agreements were not followed through and this lead to another kind of depression in mannerisms of conflicted ideological values throughout Europe. Different countries could not trust each other and thus, I think the lack of trust played an important part in the attitudes of countries moving towards war at the time.

The memorandum from one of Hitler's aide.

Hitler's long-serving military adjutant Friedrich Hossbach - seen as a major in 1934. He took the meeting notes during the secret Führer conference on

November 5th, 1937.

In the presence of many of his leaders, Hitler explained his plans to act on his external policies in trying to expand his territory. Some of his closest military collaborators were there, including one of his aides. Hossbach, his aide, wrote a memorandum the next day indicating that his words should be regarded as a testament in case of this death. He explained that the only way that Germany would be able to safeguard and preserve the nation and its growth, would be to solve their problem of overcrowding by means of force. Living space would be for the German people only, which meant that all other races would have to leave. I think this was significant because the world then knew Hitler's plans and the fact that he would use forces within his own country, meant he would not back down externally. The ideas of Hossbach attracted the generals to speed up military preparations as a way to carry out Hitler's policy on his internal and external plans.

PART 10

CHRONOLOGY OF WW II

Germany's invasion of Poland (September 1, 1939)

The Day WWII Started, this was The New York Times article at the time.

German troops invaded Poland with their drastic air attacks. The importance of this event is that the attack was given the name, Blitzkrieg, because it was so fast and sudden. This was one of Germany's new innovations for conducting air warfare. The Polish Army was forced to retreat because they were not able to handle the sudden attack and they were not prepared for it. France and Britain were not able to help and so, Poland was left between the Germans and the Soviets. Poland eventually got partitioned between the two countries. The Germans and the Soviets then signed a treaty of friendship.

The Russian-Finnish winter war (winter 1940)

One hundred meters from the enemy: A Finnish machine-gun detachment on guard northeast of Lake Ladoga in February 1940.

Russian troops invaded Finland in the winter month's temperature. The significance is that the Finland's defensive troops did not arrive on time in order to make the right plans for their strategic positioning and they were overpowered. The temperature was very cold and they were not prepared with the proper supplies as the Russians. It was obvious that the Red Army was more equipped and large enough to destroy Finland. Surrounding countries such as Denmark, Norway and Sweden, declared strict neutrality in the war. It was clear that the nearby countries did not want to participate on Finland's behalf and get crushed as well. The Red Army outnumbered the Finland troops and simply took control.

The Battle of the River Plate (December 17, 1939)

Picture: **Pocket-battleship** *Admiral Graf Spee* **enters**
Montevideo **after the** *Battle of the River Plate*.

The significance of this event is that, it was one of the first
Navel fights in the war. It was between the Germans and
British battle ships. Fierce fighting in the open sea caused
a German battle ship to go down. The Admiral of the
German ship later shot himself in the head. It was simple
to realize that Hitler's policies did not tolerate major
mistakes; this particular Admiral knew he would be in
trouble or perhaps even killed by Hitler. Even though
Germany had many fast and powerful ships, they were not
able to handle the forces of the British Navy. The
situation between the Germans and the British were not
good however, there was a standoff because Germany had
other plans to invade other territories.

The Balkan Campaigns (October 1940)

Mussolini (left) with Hitler. The German Führer had attempted to prevent the Italian invasion of Greece suspecting, correctly, that it would drag Germany into the Balkans. Italian failure in the region resulted in Hitler having to delay his long-cherished dream of invading the Soviet Union while he secured his southern flank.

This campaign was another humiliation for Mussolini, who invaded Greece in October. His plans failed and Hitler had to come to his rescue. The significance of this is that Hitler did not want Italy to invade Greece because it would cause problems for him to safeguard his Balkan flanks and protect German access to Rumania's oil fields.

Hitler needed these areas to be safe in order for his troops to be well supplied with fuel for his tanks. Hitler knew that if Mussolini invaded Greece, it would cause a threat to the Balkans. Importantly, Hitler needed the Balkans so he played as a mediator and all three Balkan powers joined the Axis.

Germany's invasion of Greece and Yugoslavia (April 6, 1941)

Microfilm-New York Times archives, Monterey Public Library

Hitler was very pleased that he got the Balkans to join axis without having to use force. The situation was that he also needed Yugoslavia to join the Axis as well. He had been trying to get Yugoslavia to join since Italy's invasion of Greece. This was important to him because he would not have to use force on them and he would use their

territories for his own benefits. Eventually Yugoslavia
agreed to Hitler but some of the officers opposed Hitler.
They staged a coup against the Germans and Hitler
became furious. This leads to Hitler using Blitzkrieg, while
sending over 650 000 troops to crush Yugoslavia and the
Greeks.

Operation Barbarossa (May, 1941)

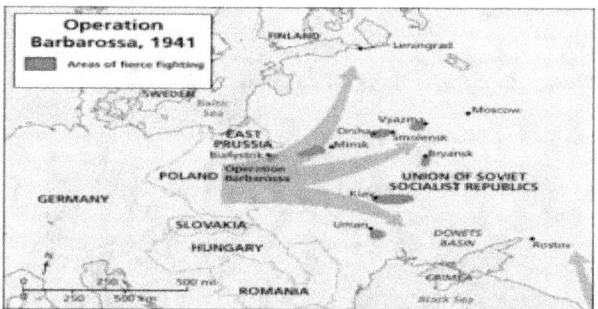

This was a situation where by Hitler sought to destroy
Russia, and take over the territories. He wanted Russia to
join his new order, but Russia required that Hitler agreed
to the terms of their territorial boundaries. This is
important because if Germany had come to terms with
Russia, the outcome of the war could have been in favor
of Germany.

Hitler realized that if he could not get Russia to comply, he
would have to use force. After hearing the terms that
Russia required, Hitler thought they were asking for too

much. He decided he would have to crush the Russians with a Blitz. Another important factor which lead to Germany's lost was their lack of resources. It was clear that Russia was more equipped in every way and this lead to the failure of The Wehrmacht's to crush the Red Army.

German siege of Leningrad (September, 1941)

The Red Army was outflanked and on September 8 1941 the Germans had fully encircled Leningrad and the siege began. The siege lasted for a total of 900 days, from September 8 1941 until January 27 1944.

The importance of this siege was that it lasted for a very

long time. In terms of days, this siege on the Soviet Union lasted 872 days. The length of this war had an extreme significant in that; German blockade claimed 650,000 Leningrader lives in one year alone. Millions of sick children and elderly were evacuated because there was not enough food supply to reach them on time. Importantly, in 1943, Soviet offences ruptured the German encirclement and allowed more supplies to reach Leningrad.

Preparation for war in the Pacific (November, 1941)

MEMBERS OF THE WAR DEPARTMENT GENERAL STAFF *(top) and the War Plans Division (bottom), November 1941. Left to right (top): Brig. Gen. Leonard T. Gerow, Brig. Gen. R. A. Wheeler, Brig. Gen. S. Miles, Maj. Gen. H. H. Arnold, General Marshall, Brig. Gen. W. H. Haislip, Brig. Gen. H. L. Twaddle, and Maj. Gen. W. Bryden. (Maj. Gen. R. C. Moore does not appear in photo.) Left to right*

(bottom): Col. Lee S. Gerow, Col. C. W. Bundy, Lt. Col. M. B. Ridgway, Brig. Gen. H. F. Loomis, Brig. Gen. Leonard T. Gerow, Col. R. W. Crawford, Lt. Col. S. H. Sherrill, Col. T. T. Handy, and Lt. Col. C. A. Russell.

The preparation for war in the Pacific was dependent on air and sea power for both the Americans and the Japanese in the Pacific. This was very important because whoever had the best ability to launch air strikes from aircraft carriers and attacks by submarines would not be defeated. It is also significant to realize that the extent of the troubles that air power posed for naval warfare had never been seen to its extremity.

With the preparation for war in the Pacific, both sides would see the affect. This is important because this event would pave the way for new interventions with regards to Air power and Naval warfare.

Japanese Bomb Pearl Harbor (December 1941)

The Japanese attack on Pearl Harbour on 7 December 1941 brought the United States into the second world war. Photograph: Bettmann/Corbis.

This event came as a total surprise to the Americans. In a sequence of events, this attack came to part after the U.S. President made final appeals to the Emperor of Japan for peace. This was significant because even thought there were indeed problems between the two countries, talks of peace by the Americans were still being presented. When there was no response from Japan some thought a Japanese attack might happen. Japan took Pearl Harbor by surprise destroying a variety of American battleships, light cruisers, and small vessels. The casualty included 2, 335 servicemen and 68 civilians killed, and 1178 wounded.

The United States Declaration of war against Japan
(December 1941)

President Roosevelt signing the official Declaration of War against the Axis powers (Japan, Germany, and Italy) in December 1941. (Library of Congress)

This event came to part after the attack on Pearl Harbor. The United States needed to take a stand and defend their territories in Asia. This was significant because the attack was so sudden and it gave Japan the upper hand. The U.S. was lead to believe that the invasion was premeditated. It was also important for President Roosevelt to state the objectives and standpoint of the United States. Indeed, he declared that no matter how long it took; the United States would win with absolute victory over Japan.

German Declaration of war against the United States (December 1941)

Hitler receives unanimous support from his Nazi Reichstag deputies during his December 11th speech declaring war on America. Below: President Franklin Roosevelt signs the U.S. Declaration of War against Germany on December 11th.

The declaration of war on the United States, by Germany, came after the major conflicts started between US and Japan. The importance is that Germany and Japan were allies and so they intended to stop and diplomatic relations with the US. Germany felt they had reasons to war against the United States. As a way to justify this, they stated that the United States violated rules and regulations of neutrality against them. Some of these rules dwelt with international law, which the United States violated. They treated and seized German merchant vessels as enemy ships. Germany concluded that both countries were at war because the US violated their rights.

Japanese-Americans sent to relocation centers (April 1942)

The Relocation of Japanese-Americans, 1942-1946. Crowd behind barbed wire fence at the Santa Anita Assembly Center in California, wave to friends on train departing for various relocation centers located throughout the United States, 1942. Photograph by Julian F. Fowlkes. Copyprint. U.S. Signal Corps, Wartime Civil Control Administration, Prints and Photographs Division, Library of Congress.

During the conflicts between America and Japan, Japanese-Americans were treated very badly. This is important because it raises many questions that deal with the entire value system of the United States. It was a significant time period because America was caught in a predicament with Japanese-Americans living there. Young Americans of Japanese descent were treated as if they did not have the same rights as the rest of the people living in the United States. Many had to relocate and families were torn apart because of this.

There were high levels of racial conflicts against anyone who looked Asian. All this came to part because America was fighting against an Asian country thus, Asian within the US paid the price as well.

The Battle of Midway (June 1942)

The Battle of Midway ends as the United States reverses the tide against the previously invincible Japanese navy

This event happened in the Pacific whereby, the Emperor of Japan wanted to destroy the U.S Pacific Fleet, a job they needed to do as a way of finishing what they started at Pearl Harbor. The Emperor knew that Japan would not be secure until it had destroyed the U.S fleets. The Flaws were that there were too many objectives that diluted Japan's strength to carry them out. Japan also face the problem of being too confident because of their power and this lead to their defeat. This is significant because this particular battle lead to a navel balance in the pacific. It also proved an end to Japan's power on the high seas. Neither their carrier force of naval air power was able to ever recover from the Battle of Midway.

The Battle of Stalingrad (September 1942)

The 1077th , an anti-aircraft regiment made up of women, is known for their fierce interception of the German 16th Panzer Division.

This event marked one of the war's great turning points and that is why it is so important. After long struggles with the Red Army, German forces found themselves in a hopeless position, they were very exhausted and in need of food and supply. At this point, Hitler ordered his troops to fight to the last man. He was against the idea of surrendering and he viewed this as a betrayal.

The Germans lost over 200, 000 troops at Stalin grad, including 90, 000 who were captured as prisoners by the Russian army. This is significant because it was a great turning point in the war in that for the duration, it left Germany trying to defend themselves against the Russians on the eastern front.

German troops begun occupying Tunisia (November 1942)

German troops arrive in Tunis in late 1942. (Private collection)

This event was a failure at first by the allied forces who did not land at the right area as a way to maintain good positioning. This enabled Hitler to send his troop into the major Tunisian ports and take them over without any major problems. This held importance because it was an event for Hitler to gain confidence about the war and maintain his policies of gaining territorial grounds against his oppositions.

Germany had been facing major problems with regards to loss of troops and supplies in Russia. Hitler needed to focus elsewhere as way to halt things in certain areas while continuing his attacks. This was the idea and the importance of the Tunisian campaign for Germany.

Germans retake Kharkov (March 1943)

A German tank damaged during the offensive.

Hitler who told his men that Kharkov should be recaptured ordered this event. It was led by General Hoth who gathered heavy armaments of the Tiger tanks that was effective against the Russian T34 medium tanks. Hoth's forces encircled and trapped the Russians in the Byransk Front and pushed on to the Donets.

This event was significant because this particular place held some importance for the Germans. It was used as winter bases for the Germans during the Russian winter counter-offensives in 1941. Hitler needed to secure this place in case he ever needed these fortified points as a place to gather and mobilize their supplies.

U.S. planes shoot down Admiral Yamamoto (April 1943)

Admiral Isoroku Yamamoto (1884-1943), Imperial Japanese Navy

The significance of this event was that of a great lost to Japan's strategic direction because Admiral Yamamoto was their chief architect for the Japanese navel strategy during this period. He was largely responsible for the development of the naval air forces and he was very important because he had previous experiences from World War Two, and had also seen diplomatic service in the US. US intelligence intercepted his movements in April 1943, and raiding P-38 fighters while on an inspection tour in the Solomon's ambushed his aircraft. Yamamoto's death was a great lost for the Japanese in the Pacific.

Rising in Warsaw Ghetto (April 1943)

A child dying in the streets of the Warsaw Ghetto
September 19, 1941

This event held significance because Germans troops had occupied this territory since early 1940. The Germans were killing as many jaws as they could in this area and between 1940 and 1942 an estimated 100,000 Jews died from starvation. The SS wanted to make the city Jew-free before Hitler's birthday which was at the end of April. This did not happen because on the day before Hitler's birthday, the SS was attacked and the Germans were forced to retreat with their weapons or die.

Jews fought Germans for the ghetto but an SS troop, which was supported with heavy artillery, reduced the area to ruins and in the period of a month, 60,000 Jews perished.

Dwight D Eisenhower named commander of the Allied Forces (Jan 16, 1944)

General Dwight Eisenhower (pictured speaking to the troops in June 6, 1944) served as Supreme Commander of the Allied Forces in Europe during World War II.

This event gave Eisenhower full command of the Allied forces. His assignment was to plan and direct the final assault on Germany. This was called "Operation Overload", where this final drive would liberate the

Continent and destroy hitter's policy in Germany. The Allied forces needed someone who would be able to lead and control the many different troops, from the many different cultures. The significance of this was that at this point, Eisenhower was already a five star general who was qualified enough to lead these Allied troops. His mission was in fact accomplished when Germany formally surrendered on May 8, 1945. At the end of the war, Mr. Eisenhower was considered the most popular military leader for the American people. He received a hero's welcome in Washington.

The Cassino-anzio Campaign (Jan-March 1944)

The first stick of bombs falling on Cassino, 15 March 1944.
Left of the Monastery on top of Monte Cassino is
Hangman's Hill. Castle Hill lies directly below

This event played an important role in the destruction of the German army simply because we saw that the Allied forces were working together well enough in order for their strategic plans to work.

The fact is, the Germans were already strategically positioned and so the Allied forces needed to attack without giving the Germans a chance to engage their reserves. The Germans were eventually caught off guard and by the allied troops and they seized and held positions, destroying the enemy's line of communication thus, taking control of the operation. Even though this event showed that the allied forces needed to work better together with the limited troops they had in Italy, the fact still remains that the enemy's line of communication was cut and they had to withdraw.

Germans surrender in the Crimea (May12, 1944)

A German soldier surrenders in 1944 somewhere in the Crimea.

This event was important in the war because it proved that the Soviet offensives were overpowering the German troops in this isolated area of Crimea. At this late period in the war, the Soviet offensives moving westward was wiping out the German troops who were lacking reinforcements, supplies, and proper equipment, all of which the Soviets were well prepared with. The Red Army was able to gain good positioning and continued their thrust against a weak and mal-equipped German army. The significance of this was that this event foreshadowed the official surrender of the entire German Army. This proved to be a victory not only for the Soviets, but also for the entire Allied forces involved.

D-Day (June 6, 1944)

Soldiers of the 16th Infantry Regiment, wounded while storming Omaha Beach, wait by the chalk cliffs for evacuation to a field hospital for treatment, D-Day, June 6, 1944. (U.S. Army photo.)

This event proved to be a significant one that was important for the allied forces to finally show Hitler that he would be defeated. The allies landed in Normandy, France, on a day that was planned for such a while now. They were certain they would attain victory because they knew the enemy did not have as much power especially in the Air. Week's prior the allies had been destroying all the enemies' line of supplies that was being transported to them by means of trains and trucks.

This event was so important for the allied forces because it was one that showed the three great powers, Britain, US, and Russia working together to destroy Hitler's Army. The fact that they have planned so well for this day was the ice on the cake for this offensive on Hitler's Fortress Europe.

Allied Advances to Paris (June 13, 1944)

M4 and M4A3 Sherman tanks and infantrymen of the US 4th Armored Division advancing through Coutances

This event occurred a week after the D-Day landings

where the Allies found themselves twenty miles inland. They all came together to form an eighty-mile front that caused the German Army to be in danger of encirclement because of the strategic positioning. Instead of a strategic withdrawal, Hitler ordered a counterattack. The Allies then took control by destroying close to 100 tanks. In this event the German Army fled as some still tried to halt the attack on Paris. The Allied forces knew that they had the upper hand and they continued their thrust in trying to reach the Capital.

For the next few days, word came to the allied forces that Paris had risen up against the Axis forces and that lead to its liberation. France was no longer a threat to the Allied forces that saw victory in France.

Roosevelt is replaced by Harry S Truman (April 12, 1945)

Harry Truman's Long Day on April 12, 1945

The death of President Roosevelt was a tragic one for
America. It came at a time where we saw the ending of
the war however; America along with the Allied forces was
still holding operations in Southeast Asia. American troops
had landed in Okinawa, Japan, weeks prior and it was
obvious that the War was still at hand because of the
Japanese Policies in trying not to ever surrender. The
death of Roosevelt made Harry S Truman, the president of
the United States. This was important because at that
point in History, it was important for America to have a
president who was qualified to handle the many tasks on
the home front and in the war operations overseas.
Truman was able to do both and one of the major things
he did on the home front was to change some of the

policies of his war department, while completing the war overseas.

Doctor Goebbels commits suicide (April 30, 1945)

Dr. Goebbels, in an official portrait. (Courtesy of David Irving, from his forthcoming biography, "Dr. Goebbels: His Life and Death".)

This event played an important role in the war because it showed a member of Hitler's clan; killing himself perhaps because of all the horrible things he has influenced Hitler into doing during the war. Doctor Goebbels is well known for his doctrines of hatred against all people other the Arian Nation (Whites), whom he considered the pure people of the world. He was responsible for spreading propaganda of hate against the Jews and many other ethnic groups, living in Germany when the war started and the duration of it. The significance of Goebbels death nearing the end of the war was important because he was a powerful man in the sense that he was able to influence many of the masses into standing behind Hitler and his policies towards the rest of the world. No longer would he be able to influence someone else who had the potential to become another dictator such as Hitler.

The United Nations is officially born (October 24, 1945)

Signing of the United Nations Charter in San Francisco on Jun 26, 1945

This was a very important event for the world on a whole. The significance of this event still holds great relevance in our society today. This event was one of the major positive outcomes of the war because it was an international event that the world needed. This was what the Allied forces were fighting for—the idea of world peace and the unification of nations in order to make the world a better place for all mankind. The United Nations hold these principles very highly because they are the basis of its birth.

All members of the UN would also uphold the rules and regulations that they had to agree upon prior to actually becoming a member. This was for the common good of the world. This was an international organization that would play the peacekeeping role for the world.

PART 11

THE WAR IS OVER

This is the world, as we know it and now the war is over.
We must all fight as citizens of the world for this reality we
need so badly. The people of the world want peace for all
who inhibit the earth. We must not forget the past and we
must continue to document history. Documentation is the
key because that is the only way we can move forward into
the future without the world destroying itself. We must try
to look at all the major issues that are affecting all nations
of the world today. This is why the idea of War, Peace,
and the common good of humanity is so important.
These are some of the major issues causing the world to be
in turmoil. We have not learned from our mistakes and
even with these facts we cannot change the world. What
are we living for? Is this what the world should be about?
The answers to these issues are not always the same and
this poses a threat to the unity of all nations. This is what
is happening around the world today and we live our lives
and carry on as if nothing is wrong. This is why these
essays and stories of different topics are to be noted. The
common good for humanity is on top of all issues so we
must grasp such ideas and hold on tight. This is not a

solution on its own as the world needs to change the entire structure of how its system works. These systems vary from the private to the public sectors at all levels and across a wide spectrum. Even though I might sometimes repeat myself, by no means do I want you to think that I am against systems, protocols, and structural development for government institutions and private corporations. I merely want to put at the forefront that we must continue to evaluate and redevelop all our systems in order to adjust to our current world, with so many customs and new cultures constantly evolving. This is why I have always made it a point to put the past and the current at a balance because that is the only way our future can be at a balance. The international community must create a mandatory mandate that suggests the ten most important issues to be resolved. This is most important for the current UN to manifest itself and create new ideologies for real targets and programs that will satisfy the masses of the world. It seems as if the UN continues to follow the wishes or the mandate only of the world powers holding seats on the General Assembly. Why should such body adhere to accepting only outlines from its members, and not set its own mandate. Such moves are needed for this body to regain the respect of the world and the honor that defines its fundamental principles. It is essential that all world leaders involve themselves in such a process in order for the common good of humanity to manifest itself in the conscience of the human race. This is what my representation of my flesh and worldly understanding upholds. As we look at the important issues of the world we must not forget that the ideas of collectivity is essential. This is the only way to effectively attack the evils of the world that creates and endorses war. This is especially important for black people who must act as the race for others to model, as they have always been showing the rest of the world that the process of peace and equality is possible. We must not forget that this is a race that brought themselves out of slavery within the past three hundred years. In knowing and understanding this truth, black people must act swiftly the same way they did during the sixties and seventies civil rights movements, to free themselves because the entire world needs them. We are not just musicians and dancers. This time and again it is for the unity of the world and the common good of humanity. This is why I say that black people play such an important role in the entire equation. The only problem is that as a race we must first unite ourselves, something that is not impossible imagining our history and how far we have come.

Many from our past Black, Whites, Asians, and Indians,

have sacrificed to make this world that we live in possible. We must not forget these great people because if we do we are surrendering to the evil that we have created. Just to name a few, we cannot forget Ghandi, Martin Luther king, Malcom X. Marcus Garvey, Bob Marley, John Lennon, Mother Teresa, Pope John Paul, and Shake Zulu. Oh before I forget, I saw a documentary in Japan, about a Japanese man who worked for the Japanese embassy in Germany. I cannot recall his name but he was responsible for giving visas to hundreds of Jews so that they were able to leave Germany and be free from the great tyrant. Even though Japan was a part of the Axis forces, we must always know that there were and will always be good men and women in all nations. The list goes on and I chose mostly black heroes because I am most influenced by them and throughout my life I have associated myself with many of their beliefs and ideas for bringing by peace within the situation of the ideal war. Even though the laws of warfare have changed throughout history, I consider these world events, as the ideal war. If we think in such fashion, the only resort must be peace. I wrote this book because I wanted to separate myself and say something of importance to humanity and this conclusion is the most difficult part. On the whole, this is how I want to be judged in life and in death. At many points I have been really stumped as to how I can end such a great cry on its written format. I can say that I know many great writers might say that they felt the same way before ending their first piece and the most important one. For me, this is the most important gift I can give to the world and I pray that many people will read my book and get the strength to make changes in the world. I cannot say that I am trying to prove just one point that my people, black people must play a bigger role in uniting the world. I am not trying to prove a point from a thesis that has been formulated to show the structure of my thought process and points covered throughout this book as being the only way and the right way. What I do know is that this book is from my heart as it is really how I see the world and I know many feel the same way. I hope that I am writing for millions who have not gained the courage to move forward and present something of such substance to the world. This is where we are together, learning from each other in trying to stop all the bloodshed that is happening around the world today. Believe it or not, my experiences of research and writing this piece were a very rough and difficult path. First I had to believe that I could complete a piece like this. It is not a novel; it is an academic piece that should be closely looked at in discussions of war, peace, and the common good of humanity. Too many writers who have inspired me to continue this book have died. At the best I had to read over many political and history books that I studied in school to refresh myself and gain strength to share my thoughts with the rest of the world.

From the many readings, I realized that my vocabulary and writing style is perhaps limited with regards to all the books that I have read. I just don't care for big world to support intellects who can mention how exquisite ones writing is from the level of technical and difficult vocabulary used. Instead, I hope that I fifth grader might read this and understand it to the fullest. This is what I want. The framework of this book is a cry for peace for the world. I have tried to show through my essays, take home exams, and historical research that as human beings, when it comes to war and peace we are going around in circles. Sometimes I feel like this point must be stressed to the fullest so I too go around in circles with the continuum of my cry. When will it all stop? I feel that the entire world has given up and all we do now is just work to pay the bills and try hard to save money for an early retirement. I cannot be satisfied with this standpoint. There must be something else out there that might help us travel through this path of life feeling that our lives mean something and we are not just here to work for a big corporation and get long vacations, end up in an old folks home, our children spending our money and then we die.

I really do not want to open up an entire can of beans but I don't consider my writing style by any means structured in any specific way. Because of such facts, I think it's ok to question my readers to think in a more non-conventional sense and therefore, branching off into a whole other issue is to me, justified. In the end I would just hope that you agree with some on the things I have said. I also do not mind if you disagree because at least then we know that some issues could be up for debate. While I am alive I consider it glorious for any man to stand up and speak his hearts desires. I consider that as long as these desires cater to the welfare of humanity, then such a man's case must be heard by the people. Here is a case I want to present while I am alive and live to see the reactions good and bad from not only my immediate circle but even more exciting from people whom I have never met. We always hear stories about amazing men only after they are gone from this earth. When they are alive we never consider them because we tend to overlook so many import issues when the answers are right in front of out eyes. I want to change that for myself and many others. I want to inspire others to try and stand up for whatever they believe in regardless of the outcome.

So what if the true glory we search for is found only in death? If this is the case then we can argue that both American soldiers and all other soldiers for that matter have a lot in common with suicide bombers and the rest of the terrorist's organizations out there. This is the idea of believing so strongly in what you are fighting for, that death is the ultimate level of sacrifice, making them the master heroes that can be achieve only in death. If this is the case that death is the ultimate glory then perhaps war is more difficult to stop. What makes the suicide bombers and Bin Laden so passionate about their cause? And what drives the American army to try and stop a force that welcomes death for the idea of a greater cause and the restoration of equality for all man. How can we really weight the two in the sense of who is right or wrong? What is for sure is that there are two sides in war and incredible forces drive them both. We have to look at both sides in its extremity because this is the only way we can come to a resolve as to what steps and plans we need to take as a society lost to the point of no return. When I ask these questions, it does not mean that I have the answers and that as you read on I will try to give my point. The fact of the matter is, I am not different from you because I really do not have answers for a lot of our social problems. What I do know is that I tend to look at the bigger picture is its final stage. Everything else in the middle is for us the people, the leaders, the scholars, the rich, the poor, to try and work together to figure out.

If you think that this is much for you it's ok, you can go and watch a movie as soon as possible. If you have not learned anything from this book then you should not be in your history, politics, or internationals class because that means that you are not interested in the class in the first place. If you can't take this to the office as a good read then maybe you are too stomped with work to ever care. Go and finish that report for the boss as your mortgage payment are overdue and the bank has been calling you every day at 730 when they know you are home from the traffic. I can understand either way because I have been there and speaking what is on my mind is refreshing beyond a cold been on a hot summer day by the beach. I am so happy that I had so many great professors who really cared for their students. They stood by me all the way and I am proud to be a Norwich grad. I was not a straight A students but I tried my best to work hard not to be perfect but to feel accomplished. With this is mind, I must also say that it was quite difficult to complete this book because looking back at all my essays and my reflections, I see a chaotic world and an American system which is essentially, anarchy.

America has always set the trends and the economic scales for the rest of the world since the Second World War, we know this. Now look at what has happened in the past and what is happening now. Don't you think something needs to be changed in the entire politics of America? Considering the facts that the world looks to America for guidance in so many things, should the big brother not act in a better manner than we have seen in the past fifteen years? I love America because it is a great country that gives hope to non-believers, rich and poor alike. It is a beautiful country of dreams where people from all parts of the world can live and work while trying to make a better life for their families. This is what the American dream is all about. I have seen it and know it is real. I have friends and families at all levels of the society who has proven that hard word and determination can lead to great success. I am not really blaming America for all the problems of the world but throughout its history we are able to see the great influences the country has had on the rest of the world. I clearly stated in the beginning of this book that we as a people of the world, we must all share the blame equally for all this chaos that is happening with the world today. Most politicians, major politicians, have passed the mid age crisis in their lives, and now politics has now become a more widely accepted field and its media representation depicts such systems with the players being glamorous and heroic. Institutions that are responsible for the rest of the world should be upheld with high regards but once such systems fail the people of the world a reconstruction must be implemented in order to restore a balance. The balance is a wide range strategic plan with various issues that the world must take seriously. As stated before the leaders of the world must come together and make a plan to tackle the ten most important issues that the world faces. I know ten might seem so little with regards to the many thousands of major problems of the world. We all know that there needs to be a starting point and a plan in order to fulfill any objective. This is my starting point for you to gather your thoughts and put these issues into perspective.

What we have learned thus far is that for the most part my essays in fact did have a similar undertone relating to the common good for the world, not just for one race. When the Tuskegee Airmen were fighting for the lives of all the people of the world as much as they were fighting for their own lives for the country to which they were born, perhaps the idea of the common good was the main moral responsibility that lead these men to victory. When W.E.B DeBois, and Richard Wright, were talking about the enlightenment, I am quite sure it was not just for the

black race but also in fact on the philosophical views of
what ought to be for the world. For the most part many
great leaders of the world did what they did with a starting
point, which is usually from a nationalistic standpoint
doing things to benefit the people of their sovereign state.
This cry for the world will bring international issues to the
forefront of what we are facing today and why see are
currently seeing so many revolutions and continued coups
around the world. All the different factions that make up
our modern technological world, are at war. Scientists are
at constant battles with worldly philosophers relating to
some of the most important issues ranging from how the
earth or the universe was formed to the idea of evolution
of human beings. We consider if the finding of what they
call the God particle is more important than the melting of
the ice caps. Does all this really matter if the main idea is
for us to prove each other wrong? This is why working
together on many different levels must always be the focus
for the beginning to the end. That is the only way great
issues will be solved. Where we are now is a long way
from where we need to be as people of the world. I might
have said this before but I will say it again. As a young boy
my great grandmother used to say that God was coming
back to claim the earth. She also told me that her
grandmother said the same thing so we gone back to the

mid-18th century. The fact is there is never a right moment to do anything. For me, I recently had the drive to write again. For some reason I am being pushed to do this by something within myself that I cannot really understand. The truth is, the only things that I really know that is solid to my heart is what I have written. We are born and we must die. The world needs peace and not war in these times for the good of humanity. I pray to the heaven that this book will be read my millions of people before I die. After my death I want to be remembered this way, regardless of my lifestyle or what I have done in my life, this is the depth of my heart and this is how I want the world to be. On the surface, I feel that nobody will ever really understand me, and what I stand for. This is what my gift is all about, a gift of truth and life. As men we live our lives never really knowing why we were born. Robert Nesta Marley, once said that his life is not his and he is living for the world and the people. This is the strong point I took. I want my life to be for the people and I want them to teach me about myself and I want them to learn from me in the process. How else can we know more about this life and why we are living in the first place? I don't believe that it matters how educated we are or how smart we are on papers, what matters is that we believe in something and are willing to die for such standpoint.

There are no real revolutionary left in this world. Fidel
Castro is now an old man and there are not many Ghandi's
or mother Teresa's left. Nelson Mandela is currently in the
hospital with the world watching and his family members
are fighting about where he should be buried. What is the
matter with us? If there are men or women with the heart
of Mandela then they need to find something to fight far.
I believe that the people of the world will be behind them.

 I want to be like these heroes who died while trying to
do great things. I am still trying to find myself but I know
this is a starting point. That is why I am writing this.
Words are so powerful and this form of expression will
always be on top for people to express their real thoughts
and feelings. We are living in a world of high technology
and I know that before I die, regular people will be able to
visit other planets, for a nice price that is. I still think the
only real religion is that of the sun. I think this should be
the only religion. Every nation and their history have
worshipped the sun. If everything started in Africa then
this must be true. The sun gives us energy to live and
plants energy to grow. We still marvel at the moon and
the stars and this is the reality I know and believe in.
Structured man made religion is just a way to control
people and we see this happening again and again
throughout the history of humanity. Aren't these issues

some of the reasons why nations are so divided? The only real thing that average people have is to travel to different countries only to experience the tourist experience and not the real essence of the country and its people. If we really think about it only a small population of the world's population has really experienced world travel. For the most part everyone is too busy to see the world and we become trapped in one place and one career for the rest of our lives. I guess that is why I enjoyed the life as an English teacher in Japan. I got the opportunity to travel and live on the other side away from North America. So far the experience has been priceless and to think that the next Olympics will be held in China, is a great situation for my life and my interest in learning more about Asian nations has been heightened because of the great friendships and love I have been given over the year from others outside of my culture. I promised myself that one day I would be able to say I traveled the world. This is what brings real life experiences to the pad on people wanting to extend their thoughts outside of the cubical and office doors.

The Far East is a great place to learn about yourself especially coming from a North American culture where we see things very differently and our brains are programmed in a very different way. It is quite interesting to look at both cultures and compare. So far I have not really experienced any major racism because for Japan, they are a really curious race and all the looks and steers are quite ok with me. What others consider racism; I consider none important in the bigger picture. For example, many foreigners in Japan claim that when they travel on the trains, Japanese people never want to sit beside them. This has been the experience of many black men and women who I know personally. A lot of times I think a smile would change all that. Sometimes we do not consider our facial expressions or presence so we need to smile at these small things and change our environments. For all changes to happen, it starts with us as individuals. Never have I walked into a place and not feel welcomed. The only issue about being here is that I think it is important for me to study the language and learn more about the Japanese culture on the whole. Language is key to it all and the fact of the matter is if I didn't go to school, I probably would not be here teaching English and learning the Asian way of doing things. I am however conflicted as to my next major move. I think it will be Thailand. They say to save the best for last and with regards to my travels I want to visit Africa last. I say it's the best because that is where my ancestors are from so please forgive me for being biased. History has also showed us that the first human was found in Africa. So I guess Europe is my next major move and then perhaps back to the far east. I never felt that I should only be in one place for the rest of my life or to have only one career to support myself. That is just not my style and I know that there are many people who would not give up the jobs and their positions to see the world. We are all different in that sense and there is no better or worse, it's just what moves us. For me, traveling the world and writing books about peace and love for the common good of humanity is the greatest thing I could ever do. So I am doing it while I am young. I am a real person with feelings and emotions, from very humble beginnings yet I have never in my life felt that I was a normal person. I never thought I was better, but deep down I always considered myself different from everyone around me. My moods are like the seasons. Sometimes I have to be the center of attention, entertaining everyone around me. Other times I want to be by myself and just reflect about my life and the things I want to do in my life. Somehow in doing that, I have always thought about others more than myself. In order to help others we must reflect on their situation and even put ourselves in the same situation. This is what my world travel means to me. I want Africa to be my last visit because I know that is where I will do most of my helping mentally and physically. I know that there are so many places in Africa that needs it but I am also a rational thinker. I want to be able to accomplish certain things in my life before I can fully grasp Africa and play my role in it all. I don't want to sound like I'm contradicting myself but I do need to feel more secured in my life in order to visit and stay in Africa for awhile. The security has to deal with many things, such as life experiences, financial freedom, and the understanding of the world and how different nations think. I believe I am on my way and that is why this book is so important for me, as much as it's important for you. It is not only a gift for you but it is also a gift for me.

So, how was the reading? Have you learned anything? We learn something new every day of our lives so learning is a continuum of our life cycle, perhaps even after we are dead, but nobody can really answer that. We can only believe. Believing in one's self is the first step in achieving anything that is of importance to the world more than oneself. This might sound weird but we are too selfish as human beings. Shearing ones thoughts is perhaps the most important and difficult thing that anyone can do. But this is the only way we can achieve peace on earth. We must continue to learn from our mistakes and from each other. Knowing and understanding must be a sheared formula for the equation of solving major world issues to stop wars from all corners of the earth. What can you do after you have put this book on your shelf? What you must do is reflect on it all and on your life. I am sure that many people will not agree with everything that has been written or what they read but reflecting on the different ideas is of great relevance. Making up stories to entertain the reader into finishing this book is not what this is all about to me. I just want to give you the raw deal about the thoughts of a man living in a world that is in total chaos. This is how I feel and I want to find a way so I write. We are all in darkness for allowing our lives to be controlled by unseen systems. The only way we can find light is to be able to understand the systems that directly and indirectly control us. Reflecting on all that is written in this book should help you to do just that. I really await the comments and reaction from the people who read this. I believe that a man in more powerful than he can really imagine. I also believe that one thought can set us free and unleash such great powers. Everyone needs a purpose for doing something, and this book is about the wars around the world, that must stop for all. It does not matter how powerful a country is and how large their armies are and the amount of nuclear power they have. After you read this book the war is over. To all the leaders of the world the war is over. To all soldiers who are fighting for what they believe and those who are fighting without knowing what they are fighting for, the war is over. This is the point. With one thought we must free ourselves and stop the war. Everything starts in our minds. Before a general sends his troops to fight he must think about it, get permission to go ahead and think again if he will live to see the end of it all. To be poetically correct, when I say man in the context of philosophical thoughts, I also mean women. And while we are on the issue, I want to say that women are the stronger half. If it weren't for women, perhaps we would have already destroyed the world with our nuclear weapons.

THE WAR IS OVER

EPILOGUE
HUMBLE BEGINNINGS, LOVE PEACE

So here goes the short reflection of the son of heaven. Indeed, we can all find heaven on earth if we truly desire and it is just a matter of a simple thought to set you free. There was always a time when I thought that I needed to do something for the world so that I will never be forgotten. I believe that a man is not just the body but there is energy greater than we know so we must search deep within ourselves to find it. It is so difficult in these times to really search deep within to fine what will make us happy. As men, we are so scared even to love. So if we cannot even love ourselves how can we love each other? Black people understand such love and perhaps now in these modern days the world knows this as well however, black people still have not found a way to unite as one people so it is very difficult for such love to penetrate. What can we as a people do to make it a reality for the world to see? Is it not time that such a revolution start again? The world needs it so badly. Each time we look at the television we see what is happening and this war must stop. We need real warriors as in the times of David. We must start thinking in terms of the great days when we built the pyramids with the great power of the divinity. Somehow some way the path will be found and this is why these words are written for you to come back to your real sense. Take these words as the gift of truth because there is no other great power than believing that the earth is the greatest energy and it can take us all in when it is ready. One does not need to be religious to take a stand for what he or she believes. Perhaps we must start thinking that the world is greater than us and it gives us energy of life. The trees are like our mothers and we are her children. I was brought up in the Christian faith and whenever we would end praying, we would say, in the name of Jesus amen. Now my way of thinking is that if we pray and we end it with, the love of the earth amen, would that be so wrong? There are so many new beginnings in our lives that we must grasp and never forget or let go. There is so much light I want to shine on you. Please read this book as it is not just a gift but it says something that ought to be told.

I was born in a place called Manchester, Jamaica. It is deeply rooted in the mountains of Jamaica and the first nine years of my life was spent in a place called, Mount Oliphant. Jamaica is the land of Ackee and salt fish, the national dish. Jamaica has great food, great people and a really great history, which gives much reference to many great people throughout its history. I grew up on the

213

mountaintop so indeed it was paradise. Today, I believe that even more with a strong sense of respect for nature and natural things. The bad parts about the place were always issues such as bad roads that the government or the local political leaders have failed to fix for years. Lately, things are getting better but there is still a lot of work to be done. Ironically, now I sometimes feel happy that parts of Mount Oliphant, remain the same because to keep paradise a love for preservation is needed. I think about such places every day of my life, the beautiful scenery overlooking Clarendon, St. Elisabeth, and its surrounding areas. There I found my wonders of the world before Niagara Falls or Mt. Fuji. How can I forget the sweet sugar cane that my grandfather would bring for my grandmother and me every evening before dinnertime? I guess to know me is to know about the place where my life started. Surely you will hear more about this special place in my heart. Let's start where my heart gave my body its first breath. My grandmother told me the story of how I was born and it was really surprising to me when I heard it. I started laughing when she told me I was born in a Taxi on my way to the hospital and she and my great grandmother, God bless her soul, delivered me. It was on the way to the local town called Mandeville, Manchester. I was a crying baby and I was told that I was very loud. This was really awesome to hear from my grandmother about how my life started and I want to continue to cry loudly but this time it is as a man, for peace for the world, so that we may all find paradise on earth.

Growing up in the mountains of Manchester was the greatest experience for Robby, the nickname given to this very curious young man. He would spend a lot of time with his Grandfather who took on the nickname Christmas. He also spent a lot of time with his Great Grandmothers' Mrs. Allen and Mrs. Emily Clarke. Growing up in the rural areas meant that there were no accesses to any form of technology so being out and about fruit picking with his Grandfather and Great Grand Mother Emily was a part of his daily activities. Emily was classical a bush doctor who had a cure for every ailment of man that we could think of. She was a master who knew the powers of plants and the effectiveness of different herbs on the human body. This was in fact passed down from her grandmother who told her stories from Africa that was passed down from the time the Maroons escaped to the mountains of Jamaica. Emily also had the ability to cure animals from their sickness as well. She was loved by the community. She was Robby`s best friend because she would tell him many wonderful stories about her elders of the past and also stories of heaven and how beautiful it

was. Robby always wanted to know more and would
sometimes go straight to his Emily`s house instead of
going to school. To know about this author, is to know
about the people who influenced him in his childhood.
His grandparents were always happy to know that he spent
the day with Manty.

Nicknames are quite famous in Jamaica and Emily took
on the nickname, Manty. Manty was the greatest person
for this young man at the time because her stories would
help him to imagine other worlds and understand that
there are other worlds beyond the beautiful stars that they
would look at . They would sit on Manty`s veranda, while
she would tell him stories of the past, rocking in her
rocking chair. She embodied the vision of a classical
Grandmother who held secrets of the earth and secrets to
cure others. It was Manty who instilled the spirit of
exploration in this young man who wanted to know about
everything. He wanted to know why things were the way
they were and he wanted to know about the other worlds
beyond the stars. At nights, the stars looked so close to
the ground that Robby thought he could jump and touch
them. As he got older he realized that it was not possible
to fly but it was perfectly ok to imagine he could. It is not
surprising that Robby now travels the world, he has lived
in Japan, London, America, and currently, Thailand. He

still continues to learn with a acute curiosity about how systems work and has become more and more interested in current global issues.

At an early age in his life his mother left Jamaica to Canada, to accept a job in Montreal, Canada. She worked for a very successful Jewish family in Hanpstead, Montreal. She was a House keeper and babysitter for the Kader`s. On her free time she would use her crochet abilities to crate amazing artwork that she presented as gifts to family members. She also went to school to learn French and other life skills. His mother was a very skilled and artistic woman who is an excellent cook with exceptional baking abilities. She is a very beautiful woman whose work ethics and unconditional support helped her son to become the man he is today. The Kader`s were very instrumental in the life of his mother because at every opportunity they gave many gifts for her family back in Jamaica. At that point, Robby was in the first grade and was very popular with the neighborhood kids. This was because of his kindness as he would always share his pencils, notebooks and coloring kits with the other kids at his school. He was known for giving away pencils and notebooks to his favorite friends in his class. He always had a lot of pencils because his mother would work relentlessly to make sure that every three months a shipment of food, clothes and

school utensils were sent home to Jamaica. Robby's father
was always a busy man and whenever he visited the area
everyone would know it was him because at the time they
would hear a motor bike or a car and his father would
honk the horn. His father was a well known police office
in the area, located in the country away from Kingston.
His father was known for dating with the most beautiful
women in the area and as a young officer with a bike, it
was very easy for the young women to be attracted to him.
He was very kind to Robby and would take him on small
trips to see the country side of Clarendon, with his
brothers and sisters. Robby has a brother Dwayne, four
sister, Keisha, Dawnette, Chyanne, and Camille. Though
his parents were never married, they remained good
friends until this day. His mother's side of the family were
the ones who provided for him and his father would try
his best to visit and spend quality time with him whenever
he could. In the later year, Robby discovered that his
father did not live in the area, and would have to go back
to Kingston to spend time with his current wife, who is
the mother of his first child Keisha, and younger sister
Chyanne.

In 1987, Robby took a plane for the first time. He and
Manty flew to Montreal Canada to reunite him with his
mother and her side of the family. He was 9 years old.

This was the first time for him to see and play in snow.
He was sent to a French school in Hampstead where he
started learning French. This was a wise but very difficult
choice for his mother who knew that her son needed to
integrate into the Canadian system in order for him to be
successful in his future. Immediately, Robby became
popular in school because of his ability in sports. All the
other children would want him on their teams because
they knew he would help them to win. This also helped
Robby to learn French outside the classroom which he felt
was much easier and less stressful. His friends in sports
really helped him at the time. Hampstead was a very rich
and beautiful community of Montreal. It was here that
Robby experienced multiculturalism for the first time. He
had friends who were different from him for the first time.
They had parents from different nations, they ate different
foods, had different religions, and had different social
and cultural experiences. As a young boy, Robby quickly
realized that he was different in terms of his classical story
book upbringing growing with his grandparents in the
Mountains of Jamaica. He knew that he was quite lucky to
have the opportunity to reunite with his mother and to live
a new life. He did however go through the ups and downs
because he was really missing his uncles and aunts whom
he knew all his life. They were his mother and his father in

Jamaica.

His first trip back to Jamaica at the age of 12 years, for was a great one. He had the opportunity to reunite with his family. It was also for the funeral of his grandfather's mother who had passed away. Her funeral was one of the greatest moments in this young man's life. He was able to meet family members from all around the world who were there for the same reason. The funeral was also the first time he experienced an open casket style event where there was a lineup of hundreds of people one by one going to kiss Mrs. Allen for the last time. Prior to that day, Robby held the responsibility with his cousin Sheldon, to paint the inside of the grave with different artwork. Because of his experience abroad the thought that this was a very historical event was very real. He thought about the things they were painting on the walls of the grave and wondered if one day someone would open the grave to once again see what was written on the wall by him and his cousin. He thought about generations in the future would one day dig to find this messages of the past. Any woman who brought 21 children on the earth, has brought a generation on the planet. Mrs. Allen was truly honored on that day. In Jamaica, funerals are quite different and though there is a lot of sadness, there is also a lot of happiness celebrating the life of a great person. This is exactly what happened.

There were parties before and after the funeral and these parties served as a great family reunion. The next day everyone would separate again saying their goodbyes and hope to meet again. The sad part about these events is that most of the time we do not see these people again until the next funeral of another elder in the family. It was important for this to all be documented so other family members, who read this, know that their feelings are the same. It is always wished the more family reunions should happen. Families become energized by these events. It is noted that he family is located around the world and have formed their own families. The cycle will continue and only the elders will know where it all started. It is very important for us to pass down our knowledge for those young ones in the family. They need to know their history outside of what they will learn in school.

I came back to live in Toronto after six years in Tokyo, Japan. I have since traveled to California, New York, and Ohio. I really love to travel. I cannot wait to see my family in Montreal and next will be the planned trip to visit Jamaica. How interesting to end this book with a sense that it is indeed final. America has a black president, President Obama; he is indeed the voice for change and unity of a people. His administration can now also be credited for the killing of Osama Bin Laden. The troops are however still in the Middle East and the people would like to know when these Troops will come home. This was a promise from Mr. Obama before he was elected into office. We will see what the future hold for a system that controls the world. Can we break the cycle?

BIBLIOGRAPHY

1.1,4,5,7,8Fogarty. E Brian, War, Peace and the Social Order, Westview Press,(Oxford, 2000), p 125,183. 2,3Clausewitz. Von Carl, On War, Random house, Inc, (New York 1943), p 53-69.

2. Paul H. Clyde, Burton F. Beers, The Far East: a history of western impacts and eastern responses, 1830-1975. Waveland Press, inc. 1991.

3.   1,4,5Scott, P. Lawrence, Womack Sr, M. William, Double V (The Civil Rights

4. Struggle of the Tuskegee Airmen, Michigan State University Press, (East Lansing:1994), p 173, 159, 235.

5.   2,7Dryden, W. Charles, A-Train-Memoirs of a Tuskegee Airman, The University of Alabama Press, Tuscaloosa: 1997, p 36, 393.

6. 6Sandler, Stanley, Segregated Skies -All-Black Combat Squadron of WWII,(Smithsonian, Press, D.C: 1992), p 133.

7. Scott, P. Lawrence, Womack Sr, M. William, <u>Double V</u>
<u>(The Civil Right Struggle of the Tuskegee Airmen,</u>
University Press, (East Lansing: 1994), p 173, 159, 235.

8. Truman<u>, Memoirs by Harry S Truman</u>, Volume Two,
181.

9. Lautier, Louis, <u>"No cause for police beating the</u>
<u>Selectees,</u>" Pittsburgh Courier, 27
        April 1946.

10. Wynne, Neil A. <u>Afro-Americans and the Second</u>
<u>World War,</u> London Press: 1970 Horowitz. Daniel,
American Social Classes in the 1950's, Bedford Books,
New York: 1995.

11. Werth, Alexander. <u>Russia at War 1941-1945.</u> E.P
Dutton & Co, Inc. New York:1964

12. Seaton. Albert, <u>Stalin as a Military Commander,</u>
Praeger Publishers, New York:
        1975
13. Leffler. Melvyn P, <u>The Specter of communism,</u> Hill
and Wang, New York: 1994.

14.   Schulman. J Bruce, <u>Lyndon B. Johnson and American Liberalism</u>, Bedford Books,

New York, 1995.

15.   Du Bois. W.E.B., <u>The Souls of Black Folks</u>, Bedford Books, New York, 1997.

16.   Wright.Richard, <u>Uncle Tom's Children</u>, Harper Perennial, New York, 1993.

17.   Machiavelli. Niccolo, <u>The Prince</u>, Penguin Books, Baltimore: 1961 ii Callahan. David, <u>Unwinnable Wars,</u> Hill and Wang, New York: 1997

18.   Paul H. Clyde, Burton F. Beers, <u>The Far East: a history of western impacts and eastern responses, 1830-1975</u>. Waveland Press, inc. 1991.

19.   *GlobalOpsAnalysisCenter.* N.p., n.d. Web. 23 July 2013.

20.   "Photos: Marco Polo Bridge Incident." *People's Daily Online.* N.p., 7 July 2005. Web. 11 Aug. 2013.

21.   Rukel. "Japan- The Brightest Hour." *Paradoxplaza.*

N.p., 6 Aug. 2012. Web. 11 Aug. 2013.

22. "File:1937 Japanese Marines Invaded Shanghai2.jpg." *Wikipedia.org.* N.p., 18 Aug. 2009. Web. 11 Aug. 2013.

23. Lochgarry. "True American Heroes: Tuskegee Airmen." *Wordpress.com.* N.p., 22 Jan. 2012. Web.18 July 2013.

24. Wilkins, Chris. "Today in Photo History – 1945: U.S. Marines Raise Flag on Iwo Jima." *Dallasnews.com.* N.p., 23 Feb. 2013. Web. 27 June 2031.

25. "Stalin's Signature Sold for $12,500." *Http://rt.com.* N.p., 13 Dec. 2009. Web. 11 Aug. 2013.

26. "Last Line of Defense." *Nysm.nysed.gov.* N.p., n.d. Web. 11 Aug. 2013.

27. "Lyndon Johnson." *Sheppardsoftware.com.* N.p., n.d. Web. 11 Aug. 2013.

28. Josephson, Michael. "WORTH SEEING: A Collection of Powerful Images of the Civil Rights Movement." *Whatwillmatter.com*. N.p., 16 Jan. 2012. Web. 11 Aug. 2013.

29. Gaster, Snally. "Richard Wright." *Buffalo.edu*. N.p., n.d. Web. 11 Aug. 2013.

30. Mack, Dwayne. "DuBois, William Edward Burghardt (1868–1963)." *Http://blackpast.org*. N.p., n.d. Web. 11 Aug. 2013.

31. Icke, David. "The US Was behind the Rwandan Genocide: Installing a US Protectorate in Central Africa." *Davidicke.com*. N.p., 9 Apr. 2010. Web. 11 Aug. 2013.

32. "GCSE History : Hitler's Foreign Policy." *Getting-in.com*. N.p., n.d. Web. 11 Aug. 2013.

33. "Soviet–German Relations before 1941." *Wikipedia.org*. N.p., n.d. Web. 11 Aug. 2013.

34. "Adolf Hitler: Rearmament and New Alliances." *Http://whowashitler.com*. N.p., n.d. Web. 11 Aug. 2013.

35. "The 30s." *Otpco100.com*. N.p., n.d. Web. 11 Aug. 2013.

36. "Hitler Reveals War Plans." *Historyplace.com*. N.p., 2001. Web. 11 Aug. 2013.

37. Karm, Bob. "WORLD WAR II BEGAN ON THIS DATE IN 1939." *Http://pdxretro.com*. N.p., 2010. Web. 11 Aug. 2013.

38. Alderin, Jens. "Trauma Portrayed with Heroism Seven Decades since the Winter War Began." *Http://finland.fi*. N.p., Nov. 2009. Web. 11 Aug. 2013.

39. "Battle of the River Plate." *Http://ww2total.com*. N.p., n.d. Web. 11 Aug. 2013.

40. "Italian Fiasco." *Thegermanwarmachine.com*. N.p., n.d. Web. 11 Aug. 2013.

41. Simpson, Homer J. "GERMANS INVADE YUGOSLAVIA AND GREECE; HITLER ORDERS WAR, BLAMING THE BRITISH (4/6/41)." *Freerepublic.com*. N.p., 6 Apr. 2011. Web. 11 Aug. 2013.

42. "Operation Barbarossa – Background." Web log post.

Hitlertriumphant.wordpress.com. N.p., n.d. Web. 11 Aug. 2013.

43. "The 900-day Siege of Leningrad." *Saint-petersburg.com.* N.p., n.d. Web. 11 Aug. 2013.

44. "THE SHOWDOWN WITH JAPAN August-December 1941." *History.army.mi.* N.p., Jan. 2002. Web. 11 Aug. 2013.

45. "Pearl Harbor Attack Remembered: 'Japan Declares War on United States'" Web log post.*Theguardian.com.* N.p., n.d. Web. 11 Aug. 2013.

46. "Remembering the Attack on Pearl Harbor 71 Years Later." *Clarksvilleonline.com.* N.p., 7 Dec. 2012. Web. 11 Aug. 2013.

47. "America Enters the War." *Historyplace.com.* The History Place™, 2010. Web. 11 Aug. 2013.

48. Yagami, Richard. "Voices of Civil Rights Online Exhibition." *Loc.gov.* Library of Congress, n.d. Web. 11 Aug. 2013.

49. "7 June - This Day in History." *History.co.uk.* History, n.d. Web. 11 Aug. 2013.

50. Lowry, Weston. "Top 10 Facts About the Battle of Stalingrad." *Warhistoryonline.com.* N.p., 31 Mar. 2013. Web.

11 Aug. 2013.

51. Evans, Bryn. "Tunisia's Toll - In 1943 the East Surrey Regiment Paid the Price." *Warfaremagazine.co.uk.* Warfare, 19 Sept. 2012. Web. 11 Aug. 2013.

52. "March 14, 1943 - Germans Retake Kharkov." *Gamespy.com.* Planetcoh, n.d. Web. 11 Aug. 2013.

53. Merwin, W.S. "Doolittle Raid 18 April 1942." *Patriotspoint.org.* Patroits Point, 18 Apr. 2011. Web. 11 Aug. 2013.

54. Bgill. *Fold3.com.* Fold3, 5 Dec. 2011. Web. 11 Aug. 2013.

55. Larson, Leslie. "Dogs of War: How Canines Helped FDR, Patton and Eisenhower Win the Second World War." *Capitalbay.com.* Capital Bay, 30 Nov. 2011. Web. 11 Aug. 2013.

56. Norton, Frazer D. "Chapter 14 — The Battle for Cassino." *Nzetc.victoria.ac.nz.* Victoria University Wellington, 1952. Web. 12 Aug. 2013.

57. "Downfall: Decline Of Nazi Germany: Crimea, 1944." *Http://historyimages.blogspot.com.* History In Images, n.d. Web. 12 Aug. 2013.

58. Moyer, Steven. "Combat Camera: D-Day, June 6, 1944." Web log post. *Http://thetension.blogspot.com*. N.p., 6 June 2009. Web. 12 Aug. 2013.

59. "Allied Advance from Paris to the Rhine." *Wikipedia.org*. Wikipedia, 4 June 2013. Web. 12 Aug. 2013.

60. Sage, Henry J. "America and the Cold War: The Truman, Eisenhower and Kennedy Years." *Academicamerican.com*. N.p., 205. Web. 12 Aug. 2013.

61. Irving, David. "Goebbels and the 'Final Solution' Revelations from Goebbels' Diary." *Codoh.com*. N.p., 01 Jan. 1995. Web. 12 Aug. 2013.

62. Santoso, Alex. "Happy Birthday, United Nations: 10 Fun Facts About the UN." *Neatorama.com*. N.p., 24 Oct. 2008. Web. 12 Aug. 2013.

NATRAWN ROBERT WRIGHT

ABOUT THE AUTHOR

Natrawn Robert Wright was born in Mandeville, Jamaica, in 1978. He is a Canadian citizen from Toronto, Canada, currently living and working in Bangkok, Thailand. He is currently teaching Business and Economics to high school students at the famous Sacred Heart Convent School, Bangkok. Robert holds a Bachelor degree in International Studies from Norwich University, Americas First Private Military Academy. He takes pride in his school for giving him a great education and an even greater understanding of the world. Norwich University is the birth place of ROTC, and plays an instrumental role in the War Department of America. It was here that the author started to learn about war and peace while developing his ideas through research and documentation. Education is very important to this author who aims to continue to develop himself in the area of War, Peace, Diplomacy and international education. He holds a Teachers portfolio for Secondary Track and continues his self development studies in the field of education and diplomacy.

For this author, traveling is the greatest experience for practical research. He describes living abroad away from his home country as being empowering and motivational. He plans to continue to travel around the world and visit

233

places that the elders of his family from Jamaica, only dreamed about. This is also a part of the reasons why he enjoys living abroad. He explains that it is not only his experiences but he feels protected by the spirits of his ancestors who watch over him daily. This author would like to continue to write books of different sort, he wants people to know him for his true heart's desire of peace upon the earth where all nations can come together to respect each other's differences and embrace the lessons we can learn from other cultures. This is what he would like to see, world peace, and equality for all nations, before he dies.